Andrea

CW01099693

A Class Act

A selection of prose and poetry from the Creative Writing class at the Tin Hat Centre, Selston.

Edited by Mike Biggs

First Published in the UK by Tin Hat Writers, Selston
E: mikehbiggs@yahoo.co.uk
TinHatWriters@yahoo.co.uk

Printed by Peppermint Books, (Part of Bayliss
Peppermint) UK

*All rights reserved. No part of this publication may be
reproduced, stored in a retrieval system, or transmitted,
in any form or by any means, without the prior
permission in writing from Tin Hat Writers.*

Copyright © 2014 Tin Hat Writers

All stories, sketches and poems are copyright of their
respective creators as indicated herein, and are
reproduced here with permission.

Copyright © of each work belongs to the respective
author. All rights reserved.

ISBN: 978-1-909655-09-6

Front cover image: Copyright: <a
href='http://www.123rf.com/profile_eskay'>eskay / 123RF Stock
Photo</a>

Contents

Introduction

A Class Act features the poems, stories and memoirs written by the members of the Creative Writing class that I have been running at the Tin Hat Centre in Selston, on the North Nottinghamshire and Derbyshire border, for some years now. All the members live in the area, made up of small ex-mining villages and towns, and I hope you'll agree that the variety and quality of the writing is of a very high standard, covering the experiences, thoughts and feelings of the people who live there. There is something for everyone here and I'm sure that if you dip into the anthology you'll find writing to entertain, to amuse, to inspire and to absorb. I'd like to introduce you to a selection.

The anthology starts off with **Mike Biggs'** pieces, including A *Class Act* an amusing and vivid recollection of a childhood infatuation with a raven-haired teacher on a motorbike! Then there's a sardonic poetic meditation on the vagaries of online dating, *Carousel.*

Claire Corbett follows with, amongst others, a celebratory musing called *My Feet,* and a chilling supernatural story about the mysterious disappearance of a child, intriguingly titled *Meccano.*

Then comes **Nicola Crook** with *Under the Bed,* a heart warming, humorous story of a young couple starting their life in the London Blitz of World War Two. Check out her memoir of childhood roaming her native Wiltshire countryside on her bike, *Real Freedom.*

To add further variety, **David Fisher** follows with the moving and tragic story of George Button, a signalman and stalwart servant of the railway. Try also his poem *Twilight,* a Housman-like paean to an idyllic pastoral scene.

Andrea Foster reveals the passionate side of growing older in *Lust Lingers* and follows up with poignant reflections about the area's mining heritage in *Colliers Wood. Sylvie's Daffodils* is a touching elegy for a local couple.

For a complete change of setting and subject matter, **Barry Harper's** vivid and inspiring memoirs take us with him on his epic trek in Canada's Arctic Circle – start out with *Aurora Borealis.*

Vince Holt's poem *A Life Not Lived* adds a philosophical air to the collection, whilst *Ticking Bomb* is a shocking micro-fiction about the heroism of love.

Local writers such as **Lord Byron** and **D.H.Lawrence** have long been celebrated for their lyrical portrayal of the local Notts/Derbys countryside. Pat Lowe joins their illustrious ranks in *My Track* and *White Peonies.*
Also take a look at her bitter-sweet comedy about a holiday romance, *O Sole Mio.*

If you like a chuckle then you won't find better than **Shirley McIntyre's** humorous poems and stories, among them a ribald tale of a young man's losing his virginity, *The Initiation*. Try also her entertaining account of the inner life of her dogs, *Dolly's Deliberations*.

Dawn Raffle follows with *The Gift*, a macabre tale in verse of her jilted lover's revenge. **Chris Rawlins** then tells us a heartening story set on the Isle of Skye, *Treasured Island*.

Cindy Rossiter's poems often inspire a wry smile in her readers. Her pithy observations on life and love include *Snake in the Grass*, about a womaniser who gets his comeuppance, and *From Here to Infirmity*, a droll look at the ageing process.

Sam Taylor tackles profound subject matter in her villanelle *I Shall Walk Alone* whilst portraying a revolutionary moment in *Gone with the Tsar*.

Yours truly, **Mike Wareham**, imagines a murderous local character in the story *Dog-Retch Billy*. His poems, all set in Wales, deal with our connection with nature and with family life.

All of us in A Class Act hope you enjoy our writing.

Mike Wareham

Editor's Note:

I was pleased and privileged to be asked to edit this anthology, and I would like to acknowledge my able assistant editors, Mike Wareham and Cindy Rossiter, for their invaluable help and support. Any errors are mine alone, and would have been more numerous without their vital contributions.

Mike Biggs

October 2014

Mike Biggs

Retired/released into the community a few years ago and now living in Selston, I had a varied career as a research scientist, sales/marketing director, head hunter and hospice ambulance driver. A dedicated 'foodie' I enjoy feasting and merriment, and write prose and poetry just for fun and fellowship

.

A Class Act

CLANG! CLANG! CLANG! The big brass handbell, wielded vigorously by the smiling headmaster, would call the children each morning from the cold, wet playground into the warm, damp fug of the school.

St Johns C. of E. Junior School, built in 1760, was a cavernous old brick and stone building with high vaulted ceilings and huge classrooms heated inadequately by large pot-bellied iron stoves at rare intervals throughout. At playtime, if the weather was exceptionally vile, the kids stayed in and gathered round the guard rail surrounding the stoves, jostling for warmth.

The stoves glowed red hot, and the boys vied to see who could land the biggest spitballs on the stove top, and watch them run around, sizzling, smoking and shrinking. This earned the spitters a clip around the ear if spotted by the teacher. In those days, of course, it was only the boys who played spitball.

All the interior walls were plain brick covered with a thick layer of pale blue gloss paint. The floors were bare dusty wood, with dark, shiny polished knots here and there, sticking up like half-buried conkers as the surrounding timber had been worn down over 200 years by scampering feet. These were slippery and lethal, and at eight years old I suffered a broken nose having slipped on a knot in a dancing class. I've never like dancing since.

Those few of us with coats, sodden from the icy rain, hung them up in the cloakroom, leaving them to drain down the glossy walls and onto the floor. We trudged into the classroom, our red noses and cheeks glowing like the burning, throbbing chilblains on our cold wet feet. Thighs rubbed sore by the rough, soggy edge of our coarse woollen short trousers, we plonked ourselves down at our desks.

A deep, sonorous roar outside sent everyone scurrying to the windows; Miss Beardmore had arrived. She rode a mighty Ariel Square 4. With a 1000cc engine this was the biggest motorcycle around; a great beast of a machine which earned her the rapt attention and admiration of every boy in the school.

Unlike the other women teachers, who were notably plain, with chunky legs like cider bottles (according to my dad), Miss Beardmore was tall, slim, and beautiful. She had a dazzling smile, bright, lively eyes, and a great mane of thick, dark wavy hair. No motorcycle helmet for her; the sight of her hair streaming behind her as she swept along on the mighty Ariel was a joy to behold.

The windows rattled as the throbbing engine boomed in the yard, and then fell silent. Moments later, Miss Beardmore strode into the room, to be greeted with instant, awed attention and stillness. No-one messed with Miss Beardmore, and that included the Headmaster, a twinkly old man in a tweed suit, smelling faintly of Hamlet cigars, and with a flat cap permanently fixed to his head. He had never been seen bareheaded, indoors or out, as long as anyone could remember.

Miss Beardmore would look around the classroom, eyeing her charges with a confident and assertive composure.

"Good morning " she said.

"Good morning, Miss Beardmore!" we chanted.

There were forty of us in her class, boys and girls, all from the local council estate, the only posh kids being those pink, chubby, cocky ones whose parents owned a shop. This made them middle class.

This was Stoke-on-Trent, 1952, a bleak and cheerless

place, with no wealth of goods or ambition; a grey, tired city like so much of Britain in the early post-war years. Our small old school, in this dark corner of the Potteries, was Miss Beardmore's chosen battleground.

She was confronted daily by a mixed crowd of children, many lacking in wit or wisdom and all from poor homes, with permanent nose-candles, vivid purple blotches of Gentian Violet (for impetigo) lighting up pale faces, and heads a-scurry with lice. Though we were often smelly, poorly clad, throbbing with chilblains all winter, and irrepressible, she loved us all, and we loved her, with passion. A perfect relationship.

When all were seated, lessons would begin, and usually within minutes I had opened a book, crept within, and shut out the world. Miss Beardmore, seeing this with her eagle eye, generally left me undisturbed as long as she could, through lesson after lesson, eventually bringing me back to reality with a gentle squeeze on the shoulder and a soft word. I was one less to worry about, being the only kid who could read properly. Seven years old, I loved her with all my heart, and swore that one day I would marry her and live a life of bliss, books and bikes. If only she had waited for me...

Carousel

Here we are in middle age, blinking in the light
Of new beginnings, former sinnings, old domestic blight.
Ready to take a chance again, tremble though we might.

Unused to brave new worlds like this we put on our best
face,
Tummies tucked in, chests puffed out, in mirror's baleful
gaze,
We strive to find our zestiness; esprit of younger days.

Everyone, without exception, playing in this game,
Is looking for the same old things; not fortune, fun or
fame.
Just Honesty, GSOH - God, it sounds so lame!

As if these things had never been in all our former years,
Through death, divorce, desertion, in life's rocky vale of
tears,
As ever and anon we try to conquer same old fears.

'Tall, good looking, Silver Fox, own teeth, own house,
own car.
Seeks lady full of fun for friendship, blah de blah de
blah...'
Translated means a chancer, shouldn't trust him very far.

'Cuddly lady, seeking soulmate' picked out from the hat,
Means daft romantic fruitcake, chubby, with a cat,
And if there is no instant 'spark', well that's the end of
that!

And so it goes. Why? Heaven knows, it's just a form of hell,
As you pay out hope and cash and time, though you know quite well,
We're just battered, unclaimed baggage on life's creaking carousel.

Footprints

As fairy gold turns to dry leaves in the light of day, so cherished memories of places past are fragile, and a return often disappoints.

It is 1990. There are four of us: my sons Dan, 12 and Davy, 9, and my pal Brian, all on temporary release from our home lives of work and school, traffic and drizzle, homework and business. Today, here in south west Cork, we are free men intent on making the most of our parole with a visit to Sherkin Island. I first came here as a student in 1965, and have kept the memory hidden like a golden treasure ever since. I feel a slight apprehension, hoping that time has not shrunk or faded the tapestry of my precious dreamscape.

A small irregular patch of iridescent greenery set in Roaringwater Bay, between Cape Clear Island and the Irish mainland, Sherkin is a tiny, glorious place. Looking west past Cape Clear there is only 3000 miles of Atlantic Ocean, with the New World on the far side. The old name, Inisherkin, from the Irish *Inis Earcáin*, means the island of the sea-pig, or dolphin.

Measuring only about one mile by 3, it has a pub, a hotel, a church and a school. Of the 350 inhabitants, most are farmers, with a few fishermen, living only fifteen minutes by boat from Baltimore but at heart a long way away. Small fields, rough pasture, rocky outcrops and sandy beaches are packed into this tiny island, with its balmy climate and profusion of life. Ancient dry stone walls define the fields, and thick hedgerows border the narrow lanes.

The small mailboat chugs gently across the choppy waters of the bay, and deposits us on the tiny jetty on Sherkin. There are no other passengers, and we are left along with several crates of bottled beer and boxes of crisps, and sundry packets, mostly destined for the hotel and the pub. A cheery local, with a huge grey beard and twinkling eyes in a nut-brown face bids us good morning and sets to work gathering the goods. Chatting awhile to this stranger, as is the norm in Ireland, we learn that the only thing of note which happened here since the great potato famine was when a tractor being delivered tumbled off the jetty into the harbour. Although it was a few years back, people still talk of it sometimes, just as they did on my last visit, twenty five years ago.

Up to date with the news, we bid him farewell and set off down the lane towards the Silver Strand, a beach on the west side of the island. Immediately the silence wraps itself around us. There are only five miles of road on Sherkin, and few vehicles. Apart from the odd tractor and bicycle, the locals use ancient cars long since worn out, with bald tyres and clapped out engines and gearboxes. Most seem to be Morris Marinas, held together with prayer and baler twine, motivated by tinkering and imprecations. The occasional clatter and roar heralds their presence, but fortunately they are few, and our walk is undisturbed, accompanied only by birdsong and the gentle hum of bees worrying at the wildflowers.

The narrow road is bordered by high fuchsia hedges, with flowers drooping over us like a myriad small scarlet lanterns. In the fields, behind the orange and yellow lichen-encrusted dry stone walls, the high shining grasses are flecked with wild flowers of every colour, and butterflies already flitter about, energised by the morning sun. As we amble along, taking in deep breaths of the rich, tasty air, we feel like kings.

Half an hour later, or maybe an hour, or whenever,

we reach the aptly named Silver Strand. The view stops us in our tracks, and we gaze wide-eyed and open-mouthed with joy. A great sweeping expanse of silvery white sand stretches out across a small bay, with the Atlantic waves distantly booming and slapping at the beach, hissing gently as they recede. It is low tide, and the sand is still wet, gleaming, smooth, shiny and untouched. In a moment, shoes and socks are off, and we step reverently onto this glorious beach.

As we walk down to the waters edge, we look back to see our footprints, like dark hallmarks clearly imprinted on the Silver Strand. We are the first here today, and this moment is ours to savour; it is just as I remember it.

The boys scamper about, exploring the rock pools populated by tiny crabs, sea anemones and the brilliant seaweeds which adorn these tiny scenes. Like the fields and hedgerows, the sheer abundance and variety of life here is a taste of a land as it once was, before intensive farming, monoculture and chemicals. Sherkin is truly a small paradise regained. Stiff muscles relax, heavy cares and worries, duties and burdens fall away, and our heartbeats slow to a gentle tick-over.

After sandwiches and lemonade, and the obligatory skimming of flat stones across the waves, we feel obliged to snooze awhile in the sunshine. Shirts off, trousers rolled up, we sprawl loose-limbed on the warm sand, lulled by the soft breeze and distant sea sounds, adjusting to the natural rhythms of Sherkin. Cradled in its kindly lap, we let our time ease gently by, and our other lives are far away, out of sight and mind. Looking back towards Baltimore, we can see dark blue-grey cloud over the mainland, but here, as ever, the sun shines, and it seems that we have slipped into another, parallel universe.

At last the sun begins to settle in the western sky. Sighing with contentment we gather our stuff and slowly wander back to the jetty, aglow with the day, to await the mailboat. Nearing Baltimore we take a long last look back at Sherkin, lying still and unchanged; my golden memories still glitter. By now the tide will have polished the Silver Strand, ready once again for footprints.

Life's little day

Sun arises, dawn is breaking,
Light steals into field and glade.
Around the world, each man is waking
From his solitary shade.

Comes the touch of warming sunbeam
Bright now, golden glowing day
Lifts the spirit, dries the dewdrop,
Chases deathly dreams away.

Distantly the deep blue mountains,
Home of eagles, soaring free,
Far off peaks, immense, unchanging,
Gird my world, diminish me.

Hard in calloused hand the sickle,
Heedlessly its sharp blade rings,
Swings its arc, relentlessly,
Marking time whilst skylark sings.

As higher climbs the burning sun,
Warm scents arise from wheat and grass,
The reaper sweats with dogged toil,
Grain shimmering like molten brass.

When dusk draws near, with body spent,
The reaper takes his well-earned ease,
Draws in the heady new-mown scents
And thrills to evening's cooling breeze.

Wheat stands vast and wide before him,
Never-ending seas of grain
Forever whispering and taunting;
Has his striving been in vain?

Sunset shadows softly spreading,
Mountains, fields all fade away,
Tired in heart and soul, the reaper
Muses on life's little day.

(After Vincent van Gogh's picture of a reaper at work in a
wheatfield)

O Me Miserum!

Oh woe, oh woe, thrice woe is me,
With angst my cup o'erflows.
(My fingers all are different lengths, and I hate my nose).
This broken heart lies heavy now,
Emotionally spent,
Deep misery dark clouds my brow,
Life's fabric torn and rent.
The stoic path is not for me,
'Tis time to share my grief,
I'll write some heavy poetry,
For handy self-relief.
A problem shared is halved they say,
So here comes my sad verse,
With haiku, sonnet, roundelay,
Villanelles and worse!
In these latter days of course,
My poems need not rhyme,
Just spew them out in dribs and drabs,
Enjambment? Don't have time...
Pouring out my inner soul,
Is ego-balm and yet...
Some people say it's adolescent,
Self-obsessed and wet!
That hurts, you know, it really stings,
I'm wounded to the core.
So back into my shell I'll
go and write yards and yards of the same introverted,
feeble, dense twaddle, and pretend
it's poetry,
and I don't care if it rhymes, is
enjambed or even remotely grammatically correct, so there!

Those in Peril

April 1941 in the Western Approaches, and a cold drizzle reduced visibility to a hundred yards. Blanketed by the wet haze, the choppy, sullen, spume-topped waves surged and fell about the ship.

HMS Eskimo, a Tribal-class destroyer of the Royal Navy, ploughed on at a steady fifteen knots, en route to escort a convoy coming in from America. The Nazi U-boats were everywhere, their relentless attacks strangling the British Isles in this war of attrition, as thousands of tons of vital supplies and many brave seamen were lost in the grim Atlantic.

Able Seaman Harry Biggs, twenty one years old, stood on the upper deck, his face blue with cold, occasionally wiping the icy drop from the end of his nose with the back of his gloved hand. Although bundled up in a woollen sweater, kapok lined jacket, balaclava and duffel coat, he was frozen to the bone. It was some time yet before the end of his watch and a warming cup of cocoa, and he grumbled quietly to himself, in the way of sailors everywhere. Top of his list of grumbles was, of course, the Germans in general and their U-boat fleet in particular. Unseen, stealthy, they could appear without warning to play their deadly game.

Harry had joined the Navy in 1938, for adventure. His mother wept and carried on when she found out, but his father, a grizzled coal miner, had simply remarked, "I hear they're goin' t'educate thee, lad." As he later admitted, he got a damned sight more adventure than he had bargained for, and today was to be no exception. A frantic shout from his mate 'Spud' Murphy, a laconic Ulsterman, made him look round in alarm. "Bridge, starboard lookout; MINE! MINE! MINE!" bawled Spud, pointing over the side, his face a mask of terror.

Immediately the Captain rang down to the engine room to slow the ship, and like everyone else within earshot of Spud's alert, rushed to starboard to see what the fuss was about. There, just ahead of the rapidly slowing ship, off the starboard bow, was the dark, unmistakeable outline of a floating mine. It was a black steel sphere, crowned with several short spikes, which on contact would detonate the 200 lbs of high explosive within.

The slightest touch of these 'horns' against the side of a ship was enough, and seeing this menacing weapon so close instantly filled everyone with dread.

The ship slowed to a crawl, and some of the men on deck turned away slowly, and tiptoed to the other side of the ship away from the threatening mine. This was pointless, as had the thing blown up alongside, it would have broken the destroyer in two, but a natural survival instinct made some recoil and seek refuge. Others, like Harry and Spud, and the Captain of course, simply watched in fascination as the mine gently floated closer, bobbing up and down, only the top few inches visible above the surface of the grey-black, icy sea. For all they knew they might be in a minefield, unmarked on Allied charts, and there could be more of the wanton mines around them. A hush fell, and you could have heard a pin drop but for the light keening of the wind, the murmur of the engines, and the soft slap of waves against the steel plates of the hull as the ship eased forwards, the bow wave now a mere white feather of foam.

As they watched, the mine bumped against the ship's side with a soft thud. Every man held his breath, waiting for the orange flash of destruction. Nothing happened. The mine floated away a few inches, bobbing and turning, its wet, wicked black horns gleaming. As the ship crept along, the mine was pulled in close again, and once more banged against the side, this time with a gentle 'clang'. Another sharp intake of breath among the crew, and a shuddering sigh of relief as once more the mine failed to explode.

Every watcher was rigid with fear; unable to move or speak, as yet again the torment returned. The ship moved gently forwards, and every few feet the mine bounced against the side; scrape...thud...thud...Now spinning gently around, rocking to and fro in the water, tantalisingly moving away ... then back again, touching sometimes lightly, sometimes with a metallic 'donk', sometimes with a harsh scraping noise which set the taut nerves jangling.

They say that at times of acute peril, your life flashes before you, but on this day, the onlookers were so utterly transfixed by the floating, bobbing horror that all thought was suspended, and it was as though time stood still.

Nothing existed but that mine softly touching the ship as it drifted by. Its deadly black spikes like evil fingertips sadistically caressing its victim.

After an eternity of pure terror, the mine finally floated free of the ship's side and into the stern wake. As it grew smaller in the distance, time started up again. Hearts pounding, the crew thanked their various gods and began to breathe once more, stomachs knotted tight, faces white with strain, hands shaking as they raised binoculars to scan the area in case of more mines.

Silently, Spud handed Harry a rifle, the trusty Lee-Enfield .303, and stood back to watch him destroy the black menace. The second shot did the trick, blowing off one of the detonator horns at a range of about a hundred yards astern. There was a mighty orange-yellow flash, and a deep 'boom' as the mine went up, to the cheers of the relieved crew.

"It wasn't a dud then," said Spud, with a wry grin. "Two shots, eh? You're losing your touch, so y'are!"

Smiling at each other, they returned to their lookout posts and the war, albeit with renewed alertness, and a certain sense of exultation. They had survived.

Clare Corbett

Aged 5, I scrawled my first story. Robust, academic boarding school preceded rigorous university (Classics and English Literature). The creative urge foundered and sank.

I taught Latin, reorganised a college library, then trained as an occupational therapist. Embracing all things medical, practical and energetic, I moved to Derbyshire and took up Morris dancing.

Joyfully retired (not grown up), I met kindred spirits. No more endless reports! An opportunity to see if I could still write something others might enjoy. Now I'm experimenting and exploring – and I love it!

First Impressions

It had to be the butterflies; myriads, swarms, clouds of them. Large, ragged and striped liked zebras; dainty, spotted and freckled; the brightest azure blue; lemon and creamy white; tawny brown lavishly splashed with amber and orange and gold. They fluttered and whirled and danced over the lavender, soared upwards and settled again, drunk and drowsy with the scent and the heat. Bees murmured, cruised from flower to flower, intent, pausing, burrowing, moving on. The hawk moths hovered more sedately, wings vibrating, delicately probing for nectar, their round furry bodies a steady counterpoint to the ecstatic dance of the butterflies.

The lavender bushes were ancient and woody, their silvery stems twisted and splitting apart. Arching up and over, lower branches trailing, they lurched from side to side, overflowed onto to the parched lawn and sprawled across the path. The sun had dried and faded the flowers to a dull, dusty lilac and grey, though here and there purple spikes still raised their heads, beacons of nectar, bright, and defiant.

The path led downwards, winding and uneven, towards the house. Rough stone, crumbling tiles, peeling paintwork, windows shuttered against the glare. A threadbare rose dropped petals, wisteria clung to the walls and twined round the window frames. Shadowed beneath the porch, the front door waited. This was our first glimpse of 'La Mouline'. This was journey's end – and a casting off, a beginning, a starting point for possibilities, for new adventures, for memories to share and store to last us a lifetime.

The heat prickled our skin, flowed over and round us

and filled our lungs. Bleached stone and gravel flung back the light. No movement, apart from the bees and butterflies. No sound, just the humming and murmuring from the lavender and a distant scratching and chirping of crickets.

All the stress and exhaustion and uncertainty of the last few hours vanished. Weightless and unencumbered, we set off down the path. Lavender parted before us caressing our ankles, the heady scent rising in waves. Dazzled, mesmerised and wreathed in butterflies we reached the door.

Voices, a stampede of footsteps, the door flew open, and out streamed my brother, my nephews, assorted family and friends. Butterflies scattered, twirling skywards in a mad fandango, or maybe more appropriately, a Bourrée. Welcome to 'La Mouline'! Our holiday had begun!

Hair

People always tell me I do a good job; well, yes, even though I say it myself, I've always taken a pride in my work.

I mean, it wouldn't suit everybody. It's a funny thing, working with hair, some people just don't fancy the idea at all. Mind you, I can understand it up to a point. Feet for example – me, I could never work with feet. Just as well it takes all sorts or where would we be?

There I go again, woolgathering – that's what Dad called it, but he was just as bad. I must get it from him, but I'm not complaining. He taught me everything I know about the trade, and more besides.

Yes, at this time of night when it's quiet and I'm about to lock up, I can look round the room and think, "Thanks Dad, thanks for everything". And I mean it, from the bottom of my heart. It wasn't something I'd planned to do from day one, it just kind of happened. I grew up helping out here and there, getting the feel of things, one thing led to another and it became my life. So - here I am.

Did I say it was quiet? It always is, this time of the week. "Quiet Wednesday" Dad used to call it, not very original perhaps, but he was always one for actions rather than words. I think people appreciated that. I mean not everyone wants to be talking all the time do they? Wednesday – yes, it's like a bit of a lull between the weekend rush, as you might say, and the gradual build up to another Friday night. Mind you Thursdays can be busy too, but not like it was in Dad's time when it was pay day and the pubs and clubs full to bursting. And of course round Christmas there's no let up – all those Christmas parties every night of the week. Still, keeps me in a job, so can't really complain.

There I go again, harking back when everything I've learned tells me to make the most of now! And I do, I do! I can look round at everything gleaming and sparkling, all my tools, as you might say, laid out neatly and in order. It's a bit like those fairytales Dad used to read to me; the brushes, the scissors, the scented shampoos and lotions. They're my magic wands just waiting to work their transformation, and each time that magic happens I know I've been able to make the day a little bit more special for someone.

There's something about hair that always fascinated me, even when I was just hanging about and watching Dad. It was how once it was washed and dried and cut and arranged, it suddenly made the person look, well, right - however they'd looked before. I've noticed that in those makeover programmes. It's always the hair that makes the really big difference, the bit that makes everyone gasp when they come out from behind the screen. Of course the clothes and the make-up all help, but not like the hair.

I learned how to do make-up as well as hair, of course, but these days I prefer to stick with the hair. I have a young girl who comes in for the make-up side. She's done a proper college course and knows all about the new brands and what works best to cover up any problem areas – how to give that natural, fresh look.

Yes, I'm a great one for everything being neat and clean and well organised; a place for everything and everything in its place. That's one of the first things I taught Jamie when he came to work for me. "First impressions," I said, "It's all about what people need when they come to us, what they expect. They need to feel looked after, so they can relax a bit and let us take over. They need to trust us, they need to know we care". And Jamie listened – he's a good lad, Jamie. Mind you, I wasn't sure about him when he first applied to be my assistant, I mean, it's not what every young man wants to do. I needed to make sure he hadn't been watching too many of those programmes on telly that make it all look a lot more glamorous and exciting than it really is. But he never minded fetching and carrying and sweeping up, he learned fast. And he's good with people too, seems to know straight away whether they want to talk or whether they just want to be left alone. So I soon let him work on his own - under my supervision of course. It's a big help now I'm not as good on my feet as I was. Standing all day, it's hard. But I'm not complaining, oh no!

He's good with children too. That's something I still struggle with, to be honest. I suppose it might have been different if I'd had my own, or maybe not. Might have had a bit of practice, so to speak. Little kids' hair, it's so fine and there's not always that much of it to style. Sometimes the only thing to do is use something that ends up making them look too old and sophisticated, or as if they were going on stage, when all the parents really want is for them to look like themselves. Only more so, if you know what I mean.

It's different with the older ones of course. I'll always remember one young girl. It was the day before her wedding and her mother had brought in her wedding dress to help choose the style – the veil and tiara and everything. How I worked on her that day! Combing and pinning every last little curl in place until she looked a proper princess. Her mother was in tears – I like to think they were tears of joy. I always say, it's a special day when they come to me – special in its own way of course.

Well, all this won't get me home for a good night's

sleep. And I've a feeling I'll be needing it. Like I said, with Christmas on its way this might be the last 'Quiet Wednesday' for a while. Last look round then; all in order, all doors locked, not a sound apart from that background humming which I never notice now. My fridge at home makes more noise, and it's a quarter of the size of the ones here.

Down the steps and out onto the street. Careful now, it's icy and the street lamp isn't as clear as usual – a touch of fog maybe. No, I reckon I was right about it being a busy weekend coming up. Turn round just once more, can't help it. There, over the door, the green letters flicker - and again I get that catch in my chest and have to smile. Light in the darkness: Funeral Parlour - Bartram and Daughter.

Yes, people are always telling me I'm good at my job.

Meccano

I felt sorry for Jake when we moved. He'd been ill for ages, missed his first term at the new school and started the summer holidays stuck in a strange house not knowing a soul apart from the family - Mum, Dad, me (big brother Alex) and Molly the dog. There was Mrs. McGilvray next door, but she didn't count, being very old and a bit mad, all flying grey hair, and eyes that never seemed to point in the same direction at the same time. Anyway, we hardly ever saw her.

The house was like all the houses we used to live in; ancient, rambling and in need of serious restoration - or blowing up and starting again, as Mum observed after a particularly trying day. There were cellars half full of water, attics stuffed with rubbish, and a couple of dilapidated sheds lurking under a tangle of brambles and overgrown shrubs. It was also several miles outside the village. Mrs. McGilvray was our only neighbour and her house, or rather her dad's (he was in a nursing home) was even worse than ours. No one ever seemed to venture anywhere near us apart from the postman and the odd lost cyclist.

But we were used to this. It's what Dad loved to do - buy up terrible houses that no one else would touch, shore them up just enough, then move on to the next disaster. Mum shrugged, coped with the mess, the upheaval, the camping in one room after another, and somehow kept a home going. She was so laid back in those days she made it all seem quite normal.

That long wet summer must have been hard for Jake. Still not well enough or old enough to escape anywhere on his own, he stomped from room to room, trainers echoing on the bare floorboards, bored, lonely and fractious, demanding food, company or attention, depending on who was available at the time. Exasperated, Mum suggested he start clearing out one of the attics.

"You want your own space, you sort it; you never know what you might find up there."

For an hour or so all was peaceful apart from the odd scuffling sound and clouds of dust drifting down from the top landing.

The whole house started to shake. With a deafening clatter, Jake hurtled down the stairs and erupted into the hall, glasses askew, covered in cobwebs and triumphantly clutching the remains of a very old cardboard box. Out poured an avalanche of what looked like scrap metal; perforated strips, plates, nuts and bolts, all scratched and faded, the odd flash of colour - blue and green and red - but overall a shifting, glinting stream of grey.

Molly fled, barking.

"Meccano!" Dad's eyes gleamed with nostalgia.

"There's a lot of it." Mum sighed.

"Isn't that a bit retro, even for you?" I said. Well, he was my little brother - I don't do boyish enthusiasm. "Great! As well as a vast wreck of a house we now own what looks like the nation's biggest Meccano collection. Bet you don't have a clue what to do with it!"

Jake glared, and hugged the disintegrating box to his grubby chest.

"Just you wait!"

And wait we did while the metallic tide flowed and spread over every surface, through every room. Random shapes scrunched under foot. Unwieldy structures lurked precariously in corners or behind doors, toppled sideways, inflicted vicious injuries on anyone within range. After a week, Mum's legs were more plasters than skin and Molly, whimpering, took up permanent residence under the kitchen table. The final straw came when Dad found a collection of nuts and bolts at the bottom of his morning coffee. Jake and the Meccano were banished back up to the attics, Molly re-emerged and for a while all seemed normal, or what passed for normal in our family. Jake appeared for meals then disappeared upstairs again. He didn't say much but seemed quite happy and was certainly a lot easier to live with.

One morning, half asleep and trying to ignore the familiar sounds of endless drumming rain outside and distant hammering inside, I heard something different. Voices! And what sounded like laughter, coming from the attic. I faced him across the breakfast table.

"So, Jake, talking to yourself now? Bound to happen I suppose."

"Not exactly..." a little smile, mouth turned down, a narrowing of the eyes. Not exactly what I would have expected from Jake. It made me uneasy.

"Leave him alone, he's just playing." Mum was always protective of Jake.

So I left him alone, but the voices were still there and I began to notice other sounds; snatches of music, sort of tinkling and a bit blurred, like an ice cream van in the distance. Eventually I climbed up to the attic, knocked on the door, turned the handle and pushed. The door stuck, swung open. At first I could hardly see Jake among the towers, the cranes, the bridges, the windmills that crowded the room. Sleek, sharp, skeletal, not exactly threatening, but powerful, watching. Smaller models glinted dully from dusty shelves or jostled for space among the stacks of boxes and battered trunks. Jake stood up and became visible, another shape, but more solid, a darker outline against the grimy window.

"How come you managed to make all these?" I demanded.

Jake did that smile thing again.

"Just practice."

Downstairs, over tea, I tried again. "You can't have made all those by yourself, you just can't."

Smile.

Glare from Mum. OK.

A couple of days later I went back to the attic, but this time I didn't knock. I'd heard music again quite clearly, as well as voices, and this time I wanted more than a smile. The light was on, not that it made much difference. Jake didn't seem to see me at first, crouched over his latest creation, a cumbersome fairground roundabout, slightly lopsided, sprouting stiff little aeroplanes and rudimentary sailing boats. As I watched, the structure began to revolve; slowly at first, then gradually picking up speed, faster and faster. Next, just as gradually, very softly at first, then louder, the music started, tinkling, old fashioned, vaguely familiar, something from an old film maybe.

Jake turned his head, smiled; the same smile, only more so, that unsettling mix of secrecy and satisfaction. And I really, really didn't like it. I think I said something about tea being ready. I don't remember leaving the room or getting downstairs. I remember sitting at the table and trying to stop my hands shaking.

"How did you do that, the music I mean?" I asked, over a plateful of shepherd's pie.

"It's a musical box. I found it in one of the trunks."

"But HOW did you build all those things?"

"David showed me." Blinking at me, a challenge.

"David - who's David?"

"Just David. He's nice. He helped me a lot."

"You don't know anyone called David. You don't know anyone here apart from us."

"And Mrs. McGilvray!" - Dad, helpful as ever.

"At least he's occupying himself." - Mum of course. I exploded.

"Aren't you just a tiny bit concerned? Jake's practically living in the attic and morphing into the Meccano equivalent of Brunel, never mind talking to someone who doesn't exist, and neither of you thinks it's the slightest bit odd?"

They both shrugged. Jake smiled.

Later, Mum took me to one side and said it was sweet of me to be so concerned for Jake, but really, children of his age often invented imaginary friends, it wasn't anything to worry about and anyway it would all sort itself out once he started school and made some real friends.

After that I started spending more time in the village. I would walk in, taking Molly with me as she seemed more unsettled recently, whimpering and shivering, unwilling to stay indoors for long. I smiled a lot at people I met in the street or in the shop, and on the whole everyone was friendly enough, although I noticed their expressions tended to change when I explained where we lived. I once tried asking about previous owners, but always got the same response - a shake of the head and a swift change of subject. The most I ever got was a

32

cursory 'It was all a long time ago, best forgotten'. So unbelievably corny I thought it must be ironic, so I gave up and concentrated on getting a life.

I hung out with some boys from my year and got to know their families, one of which included Erin. So gradually things got better, and I relaxed and stopped worrying about my weird family and my especially weird little brother.

Until the night of the thunderstorm.

It was Molly howling that woke me, rather than the thunder. She hardly ever barked, let alone howled, and certainly never howled the way she did that night. Then it was Mum, shaking me with an edge to her voice I'd never heard before.

"Alex, wake up! We can't find Jake! He's not in his room! You know he hates thunder!"

"Relax Mum, he'll be fine, probably hiding under something somewhere."

But he wasn't, at least not in any of the bedrooms or the warren of rooms downstairs or the cellars, and all the doors to the outside were locked and bolted.

The combination of thunder, lightning, howling dog and panicking parents must have fogged my brain or it would have come to me much sooner. I headed up the attic stairs with Mum stumbling behind me. The door was open - and so, for the first time ever - I only realised this much later - was the window. The models seemed to have retreated to the sides of the room, packed close together, shoulder to shoulder, spiky shapes and shadows, gleams of silver here and there as the clouds parted and moonlight streamed across the floor.

No movement. Not a sound.

In the space in the middle of the circle, squatted the roundabout; angular, lop sided, motionless. As we stared from the doorway the structure shuddered, gave a grating sound, and very slowly, jerkily began to turn as the first few tinkling notes rang out and the boats and aeroplanes began to creak and sway as they picked up speed, round and round, faster and faster in the empty room. A heart beat, two, three... the storm crashed down again, the house shook, the models clattered. Molly started to howl and behind me Mum covered her face with her hands and began to scream.

I still went back to the village from time to time; officially to see Erin but really to get away from the bungalow and everything it stood for. Mum had insisted on a bungalow - no attics, no cellars, no loft, no garage, nowhere to hide, nowhere for boxes to lie unopened. She spent all her time cleaning and tidying and throwing things away, her body tense, eyes hard. Dad was the opposite, he just sat most of the time, limp and unfocused, his tools rusting or dispersed. We didn't even talk much after the first few months had passed. That edgy mixture of hope and anger, guilt and despair had gradually drained away, leaving us numb. Molly had gone to my uncle's. She continued to howl for days after Jake disappeared, then ran away. When she did come back she stayed outside and refused to eat. I went to see her sometimes as well.

People in the village would greet me awkwardly, their expressions of sympathy suitably guarded. I could have asked questions again, but what was the point? And the police had asked more than enough questions for all of us. Sometimes I'd walk out to the house. Nothing much changed; it just looked more run down each time. A builder had bought it, tried to turn it into flats but no one stayed. Usually I felt a bit better seeing the house - it confirmed that Jake had been alive, that he'd mattered. At the bungalow it was like he had never existed.

That day, even bathed in sunshine, the house looked worse than ever. The doors and windows had been boarded up, but high in the roof the attic window hung open, a few panes still intact. Grass and weeds swayed waist high. Something gleamed in the dust at my feet. I bent down. A scrap of metal punched with holes, ends smooth and rounded, grey surface scratched and worn, lay in my hand, and meant - nothing. I knew I would never come here again. Jake was not coming back. Whatever had happened, whatever the story behind the house, or the strange events in the attic, none of that was important any more. It was over - whatever 'it' had been.

Erin would be waiting. I flung the piece of metal as far as I could back down the driveway, and turned to go.

Mrs. McGilvray stood there blocking my path, smiling uncertainly, hair more windswept than ever, eyes more erratic. "Hello Alex, it's nice to see you... I'm so glad you've come... Dad said... " her voice trailed away.

"Your dad? I thought he was... I'm sorry but I'm sure Erin told me he'd..."

"Yes, yes!" she snapped. "He died a few months ago, not long after... " her eyes slid sideways then returned, more or less, to meet mine. "He was so confused at the end, but he did say... "

Another long pause and glance.

"He said.... he said 'If ever they come back, tell them... tell them I'm sorry about the boy.'"

"Boy? What boy? D'you mean Jake? How would he know anything about Jake?"

"No... no. Not Jake, it wasn't Jake, that wasn't the name, it was... it was... David, that's it, David..."

Her fingers were clutching my arm now, clammy, insistent. She moved closer. I could feel her breath on my face. Her eyes, faded, focused, locked on mine.

Far above us came the faint creak of the attic window as it swung to and fro.

I jerked my arm free. "I have to go."

"Yes, yes..." She turned and shuffled away, humming to herself. The grass parted and closed around her as she disappeared into the wilderness that was once her garden.

Only later, on the bus on the way back to the bungalow, did I realise what she'd been humming. I could never forget that tune. Now I knew what it was. I think I'd known all along, deep down, ever since that first time in the attic. Round and round in my head it spun, louder and louder, faster and faster. My stomach heaved. I started to shiver. *'Boys and Girls Come Out to Play.'*

My Feet

I like my feet
especially in the summer,
when they are brown, dusty,
nails trimmed and tinted caramel, rose or coral.

I like them in sandals,
delicate strips of leather,
beaded, jewelled, flowered.

I like the way they tickle
in long damp grass,
or get gritty in sand.
I wriggle my toes to pick up shells.
I used to go barefoot everywhere, even in town.

I was proud of how tough they were,
on gravel or cobbles,
paddling in icy water
over barnacled rocks.

I stubbed out cigarette end with them
to show off to my friends.

I'm gentler with my feet now
but they still have to work hard.
They tap and shuffle and scuff,
beat out rhythms, music into dance.

At night they rest,
anointed with fragrant creams
chocolate and coconut, almond and peppermint,
warm, cocooned in soft wool.

I like my feet.

The Dancer

There is a flower in me -
A spray of roses, drifting, swaying
To the beat of the breeze.
Delicate and weightless.

There is a tree in me -
A willow, shivering and shifting,
Silver and green.
A pirouette of light.

There is a bird in me -
A swallow, gliding and swooping,
Wings spread wide.
Poised and graceful.

The Major Oak

I am the Major Oak; my roots lie deep in Sherwood Forest.

I watch the years pass and the seasons turn.

My canopy unfurls to the light; I welcome the rain and bend to the storm.

Far below, men and creatures scurry and meet, challenge and kill.

I know the arrow's whine, the flash of steel, the shock of gunfire,

And the dark stain seeping across the forest floor.

I am a resting place and a sanctuary.

Once a King came; cold, ragged, desperate, he reached my highest fork and clung there till the sun rose and the hunt had passed.

I remember children, shrill voices, laughter, hide-and-seek under my branches.

I remember the young men, uniforms bark brown, banded together – the Forest's namesake.

Eager and proud, pockets stuffed with acorns, they sang as they marched away.

Only echoes remain, and birdsong; but I am content.

Spring follows harvest, new forests rise in another country.

I am crumbling, shrinking, diminished despite my name,

But still chosen, celebrated, girdled with iron.

My sap still lingers, a slow pulse as my leaves drift, brittle and curled.

I watch the years pass and the seasons turn.

I am the Major Oak.

Nicola Crook

Since moving to Selston I have gained a degree, a business, two grandchildren, good friends and the joy of writing. Add all this with the support of a loving husband and four fantastic children and I would say I'm a very lucky girl. In writing, I've found my freedom and voice.

Real Freedom

When I look back I realise I had a freedom that dies in adulthood. This freedom came when my Dad gave me a rusty old bike. Big wheels, uncomfortable seat, *'ping ping'* bell and suspect brakes. I loved that bike. On it I discovered uncharted lanes, pathways and roads; a whole new world to me.

My home was in Wroughton, Wiltshire, a pretty village near to Swindon. Set in luscious countryside, with ancient monuments such as Barbury Castle, an old Neolithic hill fort, it was a wondrous place to explore.

I never went cycling with friends. Riding with them meant giving up my freedom to go where I pleased, to imagine I was on a quest, or flying an aeroplane, or just be me. My favourite journey took me up Brimble Hill at the foot of Barbury Castle, where I would sit looking at the strange lumps and bumps of the once imposing ramparts. Who had been the builders, and had my ancestors lived there? The idea that in the long distant past I could have been a warrior filled my imagination. On my trusty steed I would go in search of the enemy, or the majestic deer.

The journey took me down country roads alongside the fields belonging to the R.A.F. Back then it was used by the Royal Navy, but we always called it the RAF. Later it became host to the Science Museum, with Spitfires and Lancaster Bombers -- two of my favourites. There was also a brilliant hospital called the Princess Alexandra, which was the first to receive casualties from the Falkland Islands. When Terry Waite, John McCarthy and Jackie Mann needed much counselling after their ordeal, they came to our hospital.

As a kid and a young adult the world came to our village just because of the RAF and the hospital. It was something we were all very proud of, because children love heroes, and here were real heroes right on our doorstep.

Whizzing past all this history, present and past, I would splash through puddles, bump, skid and glide along until I came to the top of Overtown Hill. Oh what a hill! Quiet, straight and steep. I would stop at the top and wait, listening for any cars that may be about. Then, with my heart thumping hard in my chest, I would push off.

At first the speed would be normal, bearable and not at all frightening but then, oh then, it would speed up and up. I would take my feet off the pedals, grip harder on the handle bars and squeal with sheer delight, exhilaration and terror. At the last moment I would apply the brakes. Gripping with all my might, my heart would stop, my breath held, and the deafening screech of metal on metal would surround me. The main road swarming with fast moving cars would get closer and closer. I'd close my eyes and . . . to my blessed relief the brakes did their job, the bike stopped and I was alive.

Riding slowly home, I grinned from ear to ear with that sense of immortality that only a young person can truly experience. As an adult, the closest I ever came to that feeling of real freedom was on horseback, but I have long since lost the courage deliberately to brake as late as possible, just for the thrill.

Selston

"Selston," my sister frowned, "where is it?"

"Nottinghamshire." I tried again to explain to her that we couldn't afford to move back to Wroughton, our home village, and we had found a lovely new home in Selston.

It had taken me months to gather enough information to be sure that the Midlands was a good place to look for a new start. I deliberately picked places near the M1 to ensure there was a solid link to home. It was important to me and I needed to feel I could go home quickly if I wanted to.

We took the kids on weekend trips to Mansfield and Alfreton, and finally discovered Selston, just off the M1 at junction 26. When you take the Mansfield road you see a wondrous view over fields and woodlands, and snuggled amongst the scenery are the villages of Underwood, Bagthorpe and Selston. These lovely names conjure up tales of Bilbo Baggins of the Shire or Mole from 'Wind in the Willows'.

First we went to see a rented house on Hardwick Drive. It was a tiny box with three bedrooms and a garage. I wasn't too impressed when I saw it but when we got inside it was clean and tidy. We also went to St Helens church which has a reputation for being one of the oldest church buildings in the country; buried in the graveyard is the King of the Gypsies. I was fascinated by the local history. A lady was in the church at the time and she happily showed us around. Her friendliness was wonderful and proved to be another point in Selston's favour.

We nipped into the Somerfield supermarket, and for

the first time I heard the broad local accent. When the young man behind the counter said, "Alright me duck," I had to suppress a giggle. He seemed far too young to use the 'duck' word but I have since learnt that everyone uses it, young and old.

Finally we investigated the schools. We drove into Holly Hill Primary school, but quickly drove straight back out again. I don't really know why, but it just didn't feel right. All was not lost as I had the name of Bagthorpe Primary School, and directed my husband there.

The old red brick building sat comfortably at the end of Middlebrook Road. Its country location felt good, with a sense that the place would welcome my children with open arms. We tried our luck and knocked on the door, and were welcomed by the head teacher, Mr Cray, who kindly gave us a Year Six student to show us around. The children were all well behaved, and even though there was laughter and fun it was obvious they were learning too.

Before heading back to Wiltshire we let our kids have a run around the playing field off Annesley Lane. The view from there was breath-taking. The tapestry of the old cottages, red brick terrace housing, white city council housing and gorgeous mansions lay before me like a promise. On the hill stood the stone tower of St Helens church and beyond that hills, fields and woodlands offering a wonderful picture of tranquillity and peace.

"We're moving here, aren't we?" I said to Andrew, not daring to look at him.

"Yep, think we are," he said and placed a comforting arm around my shoulders as I quietly sobbed with relief.

The She-Wolf

Yellow teeth bared,
the she-wolf glares
at the lonely child,
creeping forward
quietly,
slowly,
shoulders hunched,
head lowered.

The girl looks up,
eyes wide with fear,
heart thumping
hard against her ribs,
muscles tight,
mouth open
in a silent scream.

The she-wolf
reaches the child,
sniffs her hair,
her hands.
The child slowly
unravels
her fingers
and offers
a sweet.

Surprised and hungry,
the wolf takes the prize.
The girl gives another.
Together they share,
this odd pair
sitting
in the cold damp air.

The child's warm
hand
touches her head,
stroking gently.
The she-wolf,
just an old dog,
long neglected,
lost and lonely.

The dog leaves her side,
once more part of the shadows.
The child, now a woman,
never forgot
the lonely
she-wolf.

The Shelter

"I'm worried about you and the baby," Joe said as he stroked his hand across the belly of his wife Molly. The bump squirmed at the father's touch and kicked. Joe stopped as the old inner fear came, and he looked up at the pretty face. Her bright blue eyes looked at him with the same trust and love she had given him from the very first day they had met.

"We're fine, silly." Molly smiled in the hope to reassure him but knew by the worried lines that it wasn't enough. "What exactly are you worried about?"

Jean told me you struggled to get to the air raid shelter in time," he said. The communal shelter was two streets away and recently Molly had found getting there hard going.

"She shouldn't have done that," Molly snapped. She knew Jean was worried and she had been too but she didn't want Joe to be thinking of her when he was fighting fires. The men had enough to worry about. It was her job to make sure his life was normal when he came home and he needed to know she was safe.

"Well I have an idea," he said and propped himself up on one elbow. "Since I've moved the bed down into the front room well I … will you be able to get under the bed? I have seen many saved from fallen debris by a sturdy bed. What do you think?"

"Don't be daft Joe I can't get under the bed!"

"Course you can." He got out of the slowly warming blankets and crawled down on his hands and knees. "I can get under here, you must be able to, you're only little."

"Joe, I'm eight months pregnant and the bump is bigger than you think." She looked over the edge of the bed and giggled.

"Well I don't think he's bigger than me," he smiled back up at her.

"What makes you think it's a boy Joe Forde?"

She pulled back so he couldn't see her face as the tears threatened to escape. Every day she had been praying that the child would be a girl. A girl never went to war, would never be cannon fodder. Quickly she wiped the escaping tear and scrambled down the bed. Her long cotton white nightie rode up making the going difficult.

"Here let me help," Joe got up and held out a hand. Once she was at a sitting position she looked down at the floor with displeasure.

"Come on sweetheart, at least try," Joe urged.

"Oh alright but I'm telling you I'm too big," she said and slid down and landed on the bitterly cold floor, quickly placing her blue slippers on.

"I can get under there. Look, I'll go first," he said and then with the agility of a fireman he was on his back and squirmed under, leaving a hand out. With a wriggle of the fingers he gestured her to follow.

"Joe, I'll have your guts for garters," she said, and then with a sigh knelt down with some effort as baby bump decided to play football.

"You can pack it in as well, it's hard enough without you joining in."

Once down she carefully lay on her back and turned to see Joe grinning, "Come on, love you can do it."

It felt like forever as Molly tried every angle she

could to get underneath but it was impossible. "I'm sorry Joe but your child is having none of it."

Joe's face creased with laughter as he scrambled out the other side and came around to rescue his poor wife from the cold floor. "I don't know girl, are you and the babe ever gonna do as you're told?"

"Maybe I'll surprise you one day Joe, but at the moment I'm too big. I'll just have to find a way of guessing when Jerry are sending their parcels over and then I can take my knitting and wait in the shelter before the siren starts." Her eyes twinkled at the silly notion.

"Look, I'm being serious Molls, if you hear a siren and know you can't make it to the shelter I want you to stand right next to the chimney away from the window, it's the strongest part of the house. I worry about you..." His voice cracked.

"Hush, don't you worry about me, worry about you. I can look after myself. Where we live is probably in the safest part of the city so don't go worrying about me. Besides it's my job to do all the worrying, what with you a sitting duck out there."

"Oh by the time I'm anywhere putting out fires the Jerry are long gone." This wasn't true but she didn't need to know that.

"And you think that fire isn't dangerous, unexploded bombs, dead and dying people and you're worried about little old me in the safety of a nice home. You're a daft sod, Joe." Molly playfully slapped him on the shoulder.

"Promise me you'll find a way of being safe," he pleaded.

"Yes, Joe I promise and you promise you concentrate on your job and come home to me safe."

A week later Joe had been on a long shift. The bombs had landed with more viciousness and his shift had been longer than usual. His cycle home through the abbey grounds was quiet, and a world away from the dock-side hell-hole. He daydreamed about the cuppa and toast he would have when he got home. If he was lucky, Molly would have an egg to spare from the three chickens they had in their back garden. The rising sun filtered through the trees, creating a light-show of pale yellow and warm orange. Today was going to be a good weather day, and his mood fell. A good day usually meant a clear night for bomber planes. Shaking his head to lose the image, he began to join in with the morning chorus, whistling a jolly tune he had heard on the wireless.

At the house he leant the old bike up against the wall. The blackout curtains were still drawn but he was able to peek through the letter box. At this time of the morning he would normally see Molly pottering around in the kitchen. There was no sign of her. No sign of any movement. A cold sweat came on him. Something was wrong.

He barged through the door shouting, "Molly! Molly where are you?" He ran into the kitchen and the back garden. No sign. Then he heard her.

"Joe!"

"Molly where are you?"

"In here," she cried, "Oh please…"

"I'm coming…" He ran back in the hall and into their front room.

"Molly?"

"I'm under here." Tears rolled down her cheeks as relief filled her body. She could see his worn out boots from under the bed and then his face appeared. At first he

53

looked horrified, baffled and then grinned.

"Molly, what are you doing under there?"

"You bloody know why I'm under here. It's your idea," she snapped, but with less vigour than she had planned during the night.

"Well come on girl, you can't stay under there."

"Sometimes Joe I think you're as dense as a rock. Don't you think I would have got out by now if I could?"

"But you got under there," he said, his grin widening and his eyes glinting with mischief.

"Joe, get me out of here now or you'll go hungry for the rest of your life!"

"Alright," he said. He got up and she saw his feet move to the end of the bed and then with blessed relief her shelter was raised allowing her to wriggle her poor tired body out. She started to cry.

"Hey, I'm sorry love I didn't mean to tease you." He helped her up and as she felt his warm arms embrace her she buried her face into his shoulder. "You're safe now. What I want to know is how the hell you managed to get under the bed?"

"Your guess is as good as mine," she said as she stepped back and looked down in amazement at her prison. "I heard the siren and before I knew it I found myself under the bed. But then I couldn't get out again. I've been under there all night worried sick no one would ever find me."

"I'm sorry sweetheart." Joe cuddled her again tightly and felt the protest of his child. "listen I have some news."

"Good news?"

"Yes, Dan from next door was on the same shift with me yesterday and we agreed we'd get a new Anderson shelter for the back garden. We'll knock the fence down and we can share the space."

"A proper shelter?"

"Yes."

"With beds and storage?"

"Blimey girl you don't ask for much."

"I have been stuck under a bed all night. What if the baby had decided to come?"

Joe didn't argue, he knew she was right and vowed that she would have the best air raid shelter in all of London.

David Fisher

Working in IT and raising a family used to keep me busy, but I appreciate the freedom that comes with retirement. My days are now filled with DIY, cooking, horse racing, yoga, writing and anything else that I find of interest.

Ben and the Magic Egg

Might we return forever to the innocence of youth, when magic hours and golden days conspired to hide the truth?

Ben was barely awake but as soon as he heard the noise, he was out of his bed and straight to the window. He was small for his age but by standing on the chair at the end of his bed, he could see out of the big window, which overlooked a large garden surrounded by clipped hedges and trees. Far away at the end of the garden was an old wooden gate leading to several large fields. There were no trees here to spoil the view and Ben could see Trundle Hill in the distance.

As he saw the big lorries and trailers he had heard begin to take up their positions around the field, Ben's heart began to race. He remembered when all this happened last year but that seemed an age ago. When more lorries came into view, brightly painted with jungle scenes of animals he had only seen in picture books, he whooped with delight. He knew the bigger trailers had elephants and horses in them.

His Mum came into his bedroom.

'Mum, Mum the Circus has arrived! Look, look Mum, you can see the lorries and that is where the horses live. I love the horses Mum! When can we go to the circus, Mum?'

'The circus is only here for the weekend dear and we can go on Sunday.'

'Will Dad be able to come?'

'No darling, your Dad is not due home till Wednesday.'

'Oh I wish Dad could come too. He would love to see the circus I'm sure.'

'Yes, I'm sure he would Ben, but he has important work to do at the moment.'

'Mum, how can Dad do something so that he misses the circus?'

'He would like to be here but other things are more important Ben.'

She hugged him and ruffled his hair.

'Come on Ben, get dressed now. Joe and his Mum are coming this afternoon so you and Joe can both watch what's happening in the field.'

Ben spent the rest of the morning playing with his toys and looking out of his bedroom window. He could see lots going on, and when his friend Joe came round to play that afternoon they both went down to the gate at the bottom of the garden. They watched and wondered, as the tent that Ben proudly told Joe was 'The Big Top', seemed to rise out of nowhere.

'You are lucky to have a circus at the bottom of your garden,' said Joe.

'Yes, I am, because I love the circus and Mum and I are going to see it on Sunday.'

On Saturday morning, Ben and his Mum walked through the garden gate and wandered over to have a look round and book the tickets for the next day.

'Come on Mum, perhaps we can see the elephants?'

Outside the booking tent, a crowd had gathered. They were watching a tall man juggling coloured eggs. Ben saw that they were all different colours and was fascinated. As soon as the juggler saw them in the crowd, he stopped and came over to them.

'Hello Gwen, how lovely to see you again.'

Ben noticed his Mum had a silly grin on her face.

'Hi Terry,' she said.

'Ben, this is Terry, and as well as juggling, he is one of the clowns in the circus. We met him last year. Don't you remember? You thought he was very funny'.

Ben vaguely remembered meeting one of the clowns but since this man was not dressed as a clown, he was unsure. Seeing his confusion, Terry pulled a brightly coloured bag from his pocket and asked Ben to put each of the coloured eggs, one by one into the bag. First the green, then the blue, and finally the yellow one.

'Can you hold the bag for me?' he said.

Ben realised this was some sort of magic trick so he held the bag very tightly.

'How many eggs are in the bag?' asked Terry

'Three,' said Ben.

'Well, take them out of the bag and give them back to me.'

Ben opened the bag carefully and felt for the eggs. He gave each egg back to Terry in turn but was surprised to find only the green and blue eggs were in the brightly coloured bag.

'Which egg is missing?'

'Why the yellow one,' said Ben.

'Yes', that's because it's behind your ear,' said Terry, suddenly producing it as if out of nowhere.

Ben loved this and laughed with excitement..

'Can you do some more magic?' pleaded Ben.

'Oh yes, Terry is full of tricks he can show you,' said

his Mum. Both Terry and his Mum started to laugh as well. Ben watched as Terry put all the eggs back in the bag and returned it to him.

'Look and see how many magic eggs are in the bag,' said Terry. Ben looked in the bag and saw there were three eggs in the bag, but to his amazement they were all yellow. He knew it was a magic trick but loved it just the same and wondered how Terry did it.

While Terry and his Mum continued to talk, Ben noticed the horses were being unloaded from one of the lorries. Their coats looked bright and shiny and he remembered how they had run around the circus ring, not even noticing when the acrobats jumped on and off their backs. He longed to have a horse of his own and couldn't wait till tomorrow when he would see them in the circus ring again..

'Now then, young Ben, lets see what's in the bag now? said Terry. Ben wondered what magic eggs he would find this time but when he put his hand in the bag, he could only feel some papery stuff. He pulled it out and saw these were some sort of green cards.

'Well, that's very kind of you,' said his Mum, squeezing Terry's arm.

Seeing Ben's confusion, she explained. 'Terry has turned the magic eggs into some free tickets for the circus tomorrow.'

'That's great,' said Ben, and knowing it was important to be polite he added, 'Thank you very much, Terry.'

'Well, I have some work to do now,' said Terry, shaking Ben's hand and kissing his Mum on the cheek.

'Will I see you tomorrow Terry?'

'You will, Ben. I am the Clown with the red hair that sticks up and the floppy trousers.'

Ben waved him goodbye and just couldn't wait for Sunday and the circus to begin.

Ben woke early on Monday morning. He had not slept well after the excitement of the circus the previous day, but he had loved every minute of it. The bright lights, the animals and the trapeze artists were just great and it was all jumbled up in a wonderful memory. He had screamed with delight when Terry threw a bucket of water over him and his mum. All the clowns were throwing water at each other and they had ducked when Terry had thrown the bucket's contents their way. He should have guessed it was just shreds of paper and not water after all.

Ben ran to his bedroom window and watched the activity, as the circus people prepared for their departure. The Big Top was growing smaller and someone was feeding the animals before their journey. His mum Gwen came into his bedroom.

'I wish the circus could stay here forever mum, then Dad could come and see it with us.'

'I'm sure we can all go together next year. Anyway, you're off to spend the day with Joe.'

'Oh yes, I'd forgotten,' said Ben.

'You'll be able to tell Joe all about it. Now come on get washed and dressed and I'll have your breakfast ready when you come down.'

After breakfast, Ben and his mum walked down the lane to Joe's house on the edge of the village, and while Gwen and Joe's mum shared a coffee, Ben told Joe all about his experiences of the previous day, and showed him how to be a clown and trip over imaginary obstacles. They couldn't stop laughing until Joe's mum brought them sausage rolls and lemonade.

'Have you shown Ben your new bike?'.

'No,' said Joe running towards the garden shed with a half eaten sausage roll in his hand.

'Come on Ben. It's in the shed. It's red with blue stripes and looks much better than my old bike'.

'Isn't it great,' said Joe wheeling it up and down.

'Why don't you go for a bike ride? Ben can borrow your old bike and you can take him over the fields,' said Joe's mum. Ben did not much like this plan but suddenly had a brilliant idea.

'Yes, we can go to Trundle Hill and watch the men packing up the circus. We might even see some of the animals before they leave.'

Joe, who had secretly wished he had been able to go to the circus quickly agreed.

'Now, remember boys, stick to the forest path and no riding on the roads,' said Joe's mum, 'and be back by three o'clock because your mum is picking you up later, Ben.'

Joe and Ben raced through the forest and even though Joe had the newer bike, Ben was glad he could keep up with him. They rode to the top of Trundle Hill and saw that the Big Top had disappeared, and the lorries and trailers were ready to leave. Ben sighed with frustration when he noticed that the path down the side of the hill was blocked at the bottom by some police cars, which he guessed were there to help the circus depart.

'I wish the circus didn't have to leave so soon,' said Ben

'Look, there's your house at the other side of the field!' said Joe.

Part of his house was visible through the trees although it looked tiny and Ben could not see his bedroom window but he did see the garden and someone walking through the gate. It was hard to tell but he thought it looked like Terry the clown. Joe had not noticed this and so Ben decided not say anything.

After they had watched all the circus vehicles leave, they raced each other back to Joe's house through the forest.

That night Ben was tired. His Mum came to tuck him in and say goodnight.

'Mum, was Terry here today?'

'No, of course not. Why do you ask?'

'It was just that when Joe and I were riding the bikes up on Trundle Hill I thought I saw Terry coming out of the gate.

'Oh that must have been the gardener. He's been here today'.

'I would have loved it if Terry had come to say goodbye. We won't see him now until next year'.

'No, we won't,' she sighed, and kissed Ben goodnight.

Ben felt sure Terry had been there but was too tired to think about it. He was soon asleep dreaming of white horses chasing him and Joe through the forest.

The next day it was raining and so Ben stayed indoors.

'Dad is coming home tomorrow,' said his Mum. Ben felt glad and looked forward to telling him all about the circus. Later that day, he was playing with one of his favourite toys, a remote controlled racing car.

Ben loved the car, as it swept round the armchair at high speed and spun and lodged under the sofa. As he knelt to recover his pride and joy, he gasped with surprise. Hidden behind one of the wheels of the sofa was a magic egg. He realised that Terry had caused the magic egg to appear in his house and now this would be his secret until the circus returned next year. Maybe he could learn to do tricks with the egg, just like Terry. He hid it in a special place in his bedroom, but checked every day to make sure it hadn't disappeared. Some days later, just before bedtime, he was doing just that when his Dad suddenly appeared at the bedroom door.

'Come on Ben, jump into bed now and I will tell you a story. What have you got there, son?'

'Oh er... it's a magic egg, Dad.'

'A magic egg eh?' and he took it from Ben's outstretched hand. 'And how did you come to own such a thing?'

'Terry the clown at the circus does magic tricks with them and he must have magicked one here 'cause I found it underneath the sofa. Oh, and Mum said he hadn't been here. I couldn't give it back to him, Dad, because the circus has gone'.

When he saw his Dad looked rather cross, he added, 'But I am going to give it back to him when the circus comes next year, and I hope you can come too Dad.'

His Dad's scowl suddenly changed to a smile. 'Yes, I will look forward to that.'

'Is it OK if I keep the egg till then Dad?'

'Oh yes son. Life may not always bring you the

happiness you deserve but always make the most of the magic times.'

Ben was puzzled as he returned the egg to its hiding place. As promised, his Dad read a story and kissed him goodnight. As he drifted towards sleep, he heard his Mum and Dad shouting at each other though it was so faint that he couldn't be sure and he was very sleepy. Suddenly he was filled with wonder for he was riding his dappled pony along a star-kissed pathway towards the Big Top.

Educating Rita

By dreaming spires, deep in studies old,
Languishes the teacher, to life of toil resigned.
Comes the aspirant, keen to break the mould,
Her dreams above her station much maligned.

His doubt about her chances proves unfounded.
In time their secret longings they confide.
Her First, achieved with gratitude unbounded,
Surprised, he feels a growing sense of pride.

Ties tempered with each sacrifice they make,
He finds again the lost love in his heart,
Conscious of bonds impossible to break,
Now both know they will never ever part.

As attention to life's lessons serves to tell,
Those that love to learn may learn to love as well.

The Signalman

Lives are bound by fate,
Nothing is assured.
Victims at the gate,
For them no just reward.

Prelude

In the autumn of 1922, I took up a new post as Vicar of Charfield. Gwen Button, one of the more active members of the community, was a great help, sorting out the mothers' meetings and organising many of the other church activities. Only a few weeks later she asked me to visit her husband on a matter of some concern.

On a rainy dark Tuesday evening, I arrived at the bottom of the steps to the local signal box where George, her husband, had worked for many years. For a vicar to visit the premises of the Great Western Railway was unusual so I called out as I climbed the stairs. He appeared at the door and warmly shook my hand.

'Gwen told me to expect you, ' he said and welcomed me into the warm and cosy signal box. He was a tall rather thin man and quite dapper.

'I expect you would like a cup of tea Vicar? I cannot offer you anything stronger. It's Company Rules you see. Sit in that chair by the fire and make yourself comfortable'.

I thanked him and sat down while he busied himself with the kettle.

'I hope Gwen told you that because of my work I can't get to Church as often as I should. I will come when

I get my next day off.'

'You will be most welcome George,' I said. 'I hope you don't mind if I call you George? My predecessor told me about those wooden toys you made for the poor children at Christmas. They were delightful and I hope you can do the same this year. Your wife has been of great help, too, since I joined the parish'.

'Yes she's wonderful,' he smiled. 'Gwen and I have been married now for forty five years and I don't know what I would do without her.'

While he made the tea, I looked round his domain. George was a man who maintained high standards. The signal box was clean and tidy and the rulebooks and manuals, that were part of the running of the railway, were neatly stored on shelves. Prominent among the family photographs was a picture of Gwen in her younger days. The levers that controlled the signals and points were so clean they shone in the light of the room. Various cloths hung nearby and presumably, George used these to maintain their shine.

George handed me the cup of tea and sat down. He was very smartly dressed in his railway uniform and although he had been on duty many hours, he still looked tidy. He adjusted his tie as he sat down.

'I hope I am not keeping you from your important duties,' I said.

'No,' he replied ' The 7.32 late express isn't due for another ten minutes so we have time to talk.'

I had expected him to begin then, but instead he was apprehensive and a worried look crossed his face. He sat in silence gazing into the fire.

'How long have you worked for the railway?' I asked, trying to break the ice.

'Nearly 46 years,' he replied. 'In fact it was only because I got the job as a porter's assistant that I was able to marry Gwen. I am sure her family wouldn't have allowed us to marry so young, without me having a job with The Great Western. They have been so good to me down the years Vicar. I have worked hard and very long hours but they have repaid me by giving me more and more responsibility I have enjoyed working for them more than I can say.

He was beginning to open up. 'One of our daughters was very ill when she was young and nearly died. We received much needed help from the company and fortunately, she got better. Gwen and I were so grateful and still are. I have tried to repay them with hard work and loyalty.'

'From what I have heard, you have succeeded, George. You are a very well respected member of the community.'

'Well that's very nice of you to say Vicar, but it doesn't really help me with my problem.'

'And what exactly is the problem, George? I will help you if I can.'

'It's like this Vicar, in my job, rules must be obeyed. The responsibility of the lives of so many people rests in our hands; we must follow the rules at all times'.

I could see he was becoming agitated now and I tried to reassure him. 'Well I am sure you follow the rules, George otherwise the Railway would surely take you to task.'

'It's not that,' he murmured. 'It's just that, well I am becoming so forgetful. Do you know the other day I forgot Gwen's birthday, something I have never done in all the years we have been married. Another time Joe asked me to cover for him while he went to visit his father who was ill. When the day came, I forgot all about it. At the end of my shift, I wondered what had happened to Joe. I asked the postman to find out why he had not arrived. When the postman returned, he explained that Joe's wife had become quite alarmed as she thought I was covering for him. Then I remembered. I felt terrible and had to apologise to Joe on his return. I had never let him down before,'

He looked so crestfallen and dejected while relating this, I felt sorry for him.

'Listen George, you must not worry yourself unduly. We all get a bit forgetful as we get older. Try to make notes of important things so that you don't forget them. I will ask the Doctor to pop in and see you if it would make you feel better.'

'I can't afford a doctor,' he said. 'I don't want to cause any trouble and I don't want Gwen worrying unduly.'

'OK,' I said, 'but I will mention it to him and see what he says.'

Just then there were three bells on the telegraph and George left his chair to deal with what I guessed was the Express. He began pulling various levers and telegraphing the next box regarding the approaching train. When the Express had passed, shaking the signal box in a blaze of light and noise, he returned to his levers. His tasks completed, he returned to his chair but didn't sit down. He seemed anxious to end our talk.

'Well thank you so much for coming, Vicar. It has helped a lot.'

'A problem shared is a problem halved they say and I am pleased I have met you.' I rose from the chair. 'Please pop and see me next time you are able to get to

Church and as promised I will speak to the Doctor about your problem. Try not to worry George.'

He smiled and shook my hand again while we said our goodbyes.

As I descended the steps, I wished the problems of some of my other parishioners were as easy to solve, although for reasons not clear to me then, I felt a mild sense of foreboding.

The Accident

Extract from Report by Captain Davidson into the Railway Accident at Charfield. 6th November 1922.

The man chiefly responsible is Signalman Button at the Charfield Signal Box. It was a foggy morning and he failed to observe that the goods train that passed his box at 06.55 am that was routed onto the main line had an additional engine pushing from the rear. The purpose of this locomotive was to assist the goods train up the steep incline, one mile from Charfield.

Two hundred yards beyond the signal box, this locomotive was detached from the goods train, which continued down the main line. The assisting locomotive now stood on the main line awaiting the signal to return to the goods line...

Driver Barnes of this locomotive was also to blame, because he failed to observe Rule 55 and immediately send his fireman to the signal box to report.When he finally did so, thirteen minutes later, it was too late.

Signalman Button had already accepted the 7.10 passenger train from Bristol to London on the down line as well as the 06.58 empty stock train from Darton in the opposite direction. Although, on the arrival of the fireman, Signalman Button immediately threw his main line signals to danger, the express train ploughed into the stationary locomotive at 40 miles an hour.

Both engines fell down the embankment and the front two coaches of the Express were telescoped. Seconds later the empty stock train, travelling in the other direction, collided with the wreckage and this locomotive plunged down the embankment killing the driver and the fireman. The passenger train was gas lit and the resulting fire in the two front coaches caused the death of eighteen people. In addition, 81 people were injured, some seriously.

Aftermath

Several weeks had passed since the awful events of early November. As Vicar of Charfield, I had conducted the funerals of the driver and fireman of the local train, who both came from a nearby village.

Most of my time was spent in counselling the parishioners who were involved in the rescue of those that had survived the crash.

The terrible injuries witnessed were testament to the violence of the collision and the fire. Many villagers were shocked and saddened. Gwen Button had provided her usual help at the church, keeping her chin up, even though her husband was suspended pending the result of the inquiry. The villagers wished George and Gwen well and the general opinion was that it was an accident in every sense.

Everyone breathed a sigh of relief when the inquiry found George Button not guilty of manslaughter. The circumstances surrounding the accident; the foggy conditions and the negligence of the driver of the lone locomotive influenced the findings. George was retired early by Great Western but would still receive his small pension.

Gwen was very worried about George. She told me that he had not been out since the accident and simply sat all day gazing into the fire and not saying much. George was one of the first people I had felt would need my support but because he was at a low ebb, Gwen had initially declined my offer to visit him. Now she had agreed with my suggestion of the offer of some work at the church to keep him occupied and provide the possibility of some longer-term employment.

I had knocked several times before George answered the door. When he did, I noticed how tired he looked. He did not seem particularly pleased to see me but reluctantly showed me into the dining room. We sat opposite each other by the fire. I knew this would be difficult so I started slowly.

'Gwen has been a great deal of help to me lately George and I would like to thank you for her help in these trying times.' He barely acknowledged what I was saying so I moved on. 'We have a number of projects underway at the Church and I know with your carpentry skills you could be a great help. Gwen says you don't go out much now and I thought it would help get your mind on to other things.'

'I need time before I can tackle anything like that. It's these dreams I keep having Vicar. Nightmares I suppose you'd call them. There are all these burnt people with me on a train and I know it's going to crash and I can't do anything to stop it.'

'You need to find things to do George and forget the past. You can't change what has happened.'

He looked frightened. 'The goods train normally had an extra engine and because I forgot this, all those people died. When it happened I immediately threw all my signals to red and reported an accident. When I ran down the line to help, I did manage to rescue a few people but the fire was so intense we couldn't get near to the carriages at the bottom of the embankment. Some who did get out were badly burned. It was terrible.' He was shaking now and beginning to lose control. 'I can't forget the screaming Vicar. It haunts me night and day.'

'You must try and calm yourself George. The village folk have been very kind and have helped Gwen but it is you they are missing. Many of then including your close friends Bill and Mary are very worried about you and send their love.'

'Will you promise me to come to the Church on Sunday? I know Gwen wants you to come very much and then perhaps we can look at the work we need doing.' He seemed to brighten a little at the thought of accompanying Gwen to Church.

'Alright Vicar I promise I will give it a try.' I made him a cup of tea, as he seemed incapable of doing much. When I left, he was still in his chair gazing into the fire.

On Saturday, a violent banging on the door interrupted my preparation of Sunday's sermon. I recognised Joe, George Button's workmate. He seemed very agitated and at first, could barely speak.

'What's wrong Joe?' I asked.

He spoke quickly, the words tumbling out of him like a torrent.

'A terrible thing has happened Vicar. I was finishing this morning and set to handover to Bill, when the driver of the Goods from Denton came to report that he had seen something swinging from the signal gantry at Burns Point. When Bill took over, the driver and I rushed down there. It was lighter then and we could see that it was a body. I saw it was George straight away, still in his smart railway uniform. I had heard he had not been the same since the accident, but for George to do that . . . ' His voice trailed off and he stared beyond me into the distance. I felt numb and found difficulty in putting words together.

'Have you reported this to anyone?' I asked.

'Only to the local bobby. He is on his way there now,' said Joe.

We walked to Burns Point in silence. There was nothing to say. When we arrived, the body was lying at the side of the railway line. I had hoped it might be someone else, but it was George.

'Oh dear, Joe, I will have to tell his wife, Gwen'.

I walked back towards George's house reflecting on all the terrible things that had happened since my arrival in Charfield. I brushed the tears from my eyes as I reached the path wondering how I could break the awful news.

Twilight

Gentle breezes softly blow in twilight twisting lanes,
where weary bees buzz their way, back to the hive again.
Blue skies are shot with pink and gold, as sunlight slowly
wanes.
Jets departed feathered traces, all that now remain.

An old red tractor, dormant, still, its hard day's work
complete.
Across brown fields lie straight edged scars of furrows
neatly scored.
Lone rooks and crows still scout the fields, amongst the
severed wheat.
Now in darkness, hardly seen, the black wrapped bales lie
stored.

Forgotten toys and bikes left scattered, 'midst the broken
flowers,
as children whisper secrets low, before they fall asleep.
Church bells chime the day away, as bats sweep lonely
towers.
Deep shadows lengthen on the green where hedgehogs
start to creep.

The Rose and Crown, a lofty beacon, shuns the fading
light.
Inside there's talk and banter on how they played the
game,
and when Jim won it with that catch, it really was a sight!
Borne off the field in triumph. Will he ever be the same?

Led in from deepening darkness, walk weary horses
steaming.
The stable lights now beckon, with smells of oats and
hay.
Young grooms brush with vigour; now horses' coats are
gleaming,
their work all done take pathways home, the dog to show
the way.

The last rays of the sun depart behind the broken wall,
The owl begins his vigil and hoots a lonely tune.
The day is done, the shadows gone; will darkness cover
all?
but then, across the dimming sky, now bright the rising
moon.

Andrea Foster

In my life I've performed many roles; some to be proud of and some best forgotten! I have been variously a dancer, mother, social worker, lecturer and many other things in between. Now I'm retired, with time to ponder the intricacies of a life well and truly lived, whilst actively seeking new opportunities and experiences

Colliers Wood

Ghostly figures watch in awe; 'breathe the fresh air' they whisper. Trees sway as spirits of the past soar above, swirling the leaves and branches into a frenzy.

Spectres look down in wonder at the dramatic change. Where are the dark dusty coal wagons groaning and clanking as metal meets chain? Where are the whistles of engines, the cacophony of sounds, screaming in defiance, each louder than the other?

Where are the men with bowed backs, black-lined eyes staring from grey sullen faces; those generations of men destined to toil in darkness in the bowels of the earth?

King Coal is dead!

The mud-strewn tracks once trudged daily by workers, are now transformed into clean pathways and open spaces for others to roam. Meadows of cornflower and buttercup, where birds sing their song of freedom, replace the doomed caged canary. Wildfowl silently gliding across the lake leave a stream of chevron ripples in their wake.

Nature at peace is allowed to flourish to conceal the lives of brave men and boys who toiled in a living black hell.

Ghostly whispers murmur on and smile at their legacy. 'Breathe the fresh air and remember… remember the price we paid.'

Lust Lingers

Oh! How I could love you dear, dear boy,
Were it not I lived so long in years.
Oh! Handsome youth such delights to enjoy
As the moon-tides ebb and flow my fancied fears.

My swelling heart then crashes, wave on shore,
Your enigmatic smile speaks hints of pleasure.
My spirits rise as a river's tidal bore
Soaring, majestic, engorged by manly measure.

But the fantasies of love are never lost; I lust, I dream
From afar of wonders known but never shall again.
False passion's borne away on time's swift stream,
Yet we are as dead without desire to yearn.

Be still my breathless heart and lustful loins, I say yet;
Love is life and life is love, and living never must we
forget.

Off to War

Be glad for me mother, away from the pit,
from the dark dank misery of underground life.
No more lungs clogged with coal dust,
nor days without light.
Now I can breathe the fresh air.

Be proud of me mother, how smart I look,
a private marching with Pals!
Take the shilling, serve the King,
'Your country needs you,' the posters proclaim.
Now I can hear the birdsong.

Don't fear for me mother, I long to go
across the sea to another land.
Away from meadows of green and gold
to fields where blood red poppies stand.
Now I can smell the roses.

Don't weep for me mother, no longer a boy,
your love of sixteen years my strength.
Day breaks, sun sets for you as for me,
stars shine in the same night sky.
Now I can feel the rain on my face.

Be glad for me mother … I'm off to war.

Sylvie's Daffodils

Swaying in sunshine proud, strong,
green and yellow flashes of light.
Year after year a balletic dance
emerges from darkness to reunite.

Planted at her request by him,
knowing soon she'd be gone.
To commemorate our life together she said,
to remember me by … her swansong.

Once winter passed he'd look for signs,
little shoots of hope emerging.
Symbols of their endless love,
then tearfully sigh, memories resurging.

Life without her was hard to bear,
loneliness, depression, ill health his soul-mate.
'What's the point' became his mantra,
a broken heart defined his fate.

Spring is here and again they dance,
undeterred by frost and snow.
The sale board says there may be change;
will this become their final show?

The Folder

A folder in an old oak wardrobe,
With musty smell of parlours,
candles, coal fires and tobacco smoke,
Dog-eared faded pages, memories,
dates, events, newspaper cuttings.
Black and white photographs;
a grinning young man rides a bike,
a soldier stands proudly with comrades
on some distant shore.
War medals faded, ribbons discoloured.

His story unfolds;
black and white snaps of his wedding,
children at play in a garden.
Sepia pictures of his long dead parents posing stiffly,
grandparents in formal dress
staring dispassionately at the camera.
Ninety years preserved in a dingy folder
carefully made by work-weary hands,
a legacy of a humble man
prepared to share his journey.
A folder no one cares to see…

The Photo

Sibling rivalry forgotten,
a moment frozen in time.
Innocents, unaware, smiling into the camera.
What became of the bright eyed,
mischievous, fun-loving boy
who followed me everywhere?
"Take your brother with you" my mam said.

Days spent trekking in the woods.
Games by the river, steam train names,
numbers scribbled in a book, bluebell picking.
You got lost following me to the bluebell wood.
I didn't listen when mam said, "Take your brother with
you."
Oh, the relief when you turned up
proudly carrying two bluebells,
your fat little legs frantically pedalling a three wheeler
bike .
We broke Dad's ruler whilst arguing,
then blamed each other,
and we both got a hefty smack.
Then bonded together by the injustice of it.

I tried to shake you off
when I got my first boyfriend,
and you sneaked up with a big grin saying,
"Mam says you've got to take me with you."

Life as young adults was exciting,
No mam saying, "Take your brother with you".
We both believed the myth
that 'Love is all you need.'

Is this where it all went wrong?
Is this when the demons came, with silent stealth?
'Love, love, love,' the Beatles sang, yet it evaded you.
What love you found was quickly lost.
Darkness and despair followed two failed marriages.

You promised yourself success before thirty.
What did success mean to you?
The simple things: a family, a home, a worthwhile career?
One out of three wasn't enough
for your fragile sense of self.

What went through your mind when you sat alone
smoking a cigarette in the front of your beloved TR2?
Were you listening to music, thinking about life,
about your perceived failings?
Was it a cry for help, a cry unheeded?
A tragic mistake?

I'll never know,
nor have the chance to say goodbye.
Yet comfort came in a dream,
a cheerful, carefree, confident you saying,
"Don't worry sis,"

"Take your brother with you," mam said.
She was right.

I'll always take you with me.

Who's that man?

I'm sitting at the big square wooden table in the kitchen of Nana and Grandda's house. My cousin Geoff and I are playing 'I-Spy', Nana's baking bread, and the smell from the oven is making my mouth water. I watch as she folds a tea towel in two, and opens the door of the shiny black-leaded range. Her face is red from the fire and there are small drops of sweat on her forehead, making her hair fall into little curls around her face.

Out of the oven she takes one, two, three loaves of bread, all baked to perfection with crusty brown tops spilling over the sides of the baking tins. I watch her tip each loaf into the tea towel, knock it on its bottom with her knuckles, and listen for the hollow sound which says it's cooked, then place them in a neat row on the cooling rack on the end of the table. She wipes her hands and replaces her flour covered pinny with a clean one. I have watched her do this many times and know I have to be patient!

After what seems an age she slices the crust off the end of a loaf, slathers it with butter whilst it's still warm, and with a wink of her eye gives Geoff and me a piece. This is the treat we've been waiting for, and eat with delight as the butter seeps through our fingers and lingers on our lips. We silently munch away until the last crumb is eaten and each finger licked clean.

It's always cosy in Nana's kitchen, but today with the lovely smell of fresh-baked bread, and a warm orange glow from the fire, it feels extra snug. The kettle sitting on the hob hisses and pops as the boiling water lifts the lid, and drops it again. I start to feel sleepy and my eyelids grow heavy.

Suddenly I wake with a jolt! There's a noise at the

back door and I can hear loud voices shouting over each other. I hear my Nana screech, "Eeh well! Come in pet." Looking up, I see a tall man standing there with his arms around my mam.

She's crying and laughing at the same time, and she's wearing her new dress which she says is only for best! The man has dark brown hair and a very brown face. Not quite as brown as the Indian man with a turban who comes round the houses selling things from his suitcase, but still very brown.

I don't like all this noise; the house is usually quiet at this time of day, especially when my Grandda's in bed after the night shift; if they wake him he'll be vexed and start shouting. I look closer at the man and see he's in a khaki uniform like Uncle Eddie and Uncle Jo used to wear. He's thrown a big canvas bag, which I know is called a kit bag, on the floor near the back door and it rolls slowly across the flagstones of the scullery.

Leaving the table, I creep towards Nana, peering from behind her skirt to have a better look. I don't like the way my mam is snuggling up to this man; there's something not right!

I decide to go upstairs to get away from the noise, but the stairs are blocked by my Grandda, who comes running down in his shirt and trousers, braces flapping wildly. "What's gannin on, and who's making all that bloody noise?" he shouts angrily.

"It's Bobby, dad; he's back," mam replies.

"Well, tell the bugger to make less noise! Some of us have to gan to work the night, tha kna's."

Grandda's in a bad mood; I knew he would be. I hear him muttering under his breath, "Back is he? I suppose he thinks he's won the bloody war single handed!"

Then he snatches his packet of Woodbines and a box of matches from the mantelpiece, goes out to the yard and slams the door as he shuts himself in the lavvy.

Nana is lining up cups and pouring out tea. I touch her hand and whisper, "I don't think Grandda likes that man."

"Shush, pet, never you mind, " she replies softly.

'I don't think I do either,' I say quietly to myself.

My mam and the man are now on the rocking chair, and she's sitting on his knee. I've never seen her look so happy; her eyes are sparkling, and she's smiling and giggling as she kisses the man on his face and neck. This looks strange, and I watch in silence, unable to understand. Mam then reaches her hand out to me, saying "Come on pet, have a cuddle,"

"No, no. I don't want to!" I say, and run back to the table.

My cousin Geoff, who's older than me, then jumps up and runs towards the man, shouting excitedly, "I know, it's Uncle Bobby isn't it? Come back from the war." He leaps onto the rocking chair, joining in the jumble of cuddles and kisses. I'm angry at Geoff. He isn't supposed to like this man; I don't. And why call him Uncle Bobby? I have four uncles, and none of them are called Bobby.

Nana tries to pull me from the table and push me towards the chair, where the three bodies are tangled, laughing like mad. "Come on, don't be silly," she says. The noise is getting louder, and, frightened, I start to cry, although not sure why. Grandda comes back from the yard shouting "Leave the bairn. Can't you see you're upsetting her?" He picks me up in his arms and carries me towards the stairs. "We're away to bed, and you buggers had better keep the noise down!" he says.

Eventually I fall asleep feeling snug and safe with Grandda, hoping that things will return to normal when I wake, and that the strange man downstairs causing all the trouble will have gone. Of course this doesn't happen, as my small, secure little world has changed forever.

And that's how I met my dad. He was posted to Burma when I was just a few days old, and returned three years later. I refused to call him Daddy. I couldn't understand why Geoff called him Uncle Bobby, so my little mind compromised, and to me he became Daddy Bobby.

Barry Harper

A retired Police Officer, I worked for thirty-two years in Nottinghamshire Police and now work part-time for a Danish security company, and teach primary school children about the dangers of drugs, alcohol, tobacco and bullying. I am a keen sportsman and play the saxophone, and am learning the craft of writing stories that people want to read.

A Majestic stand-off

Whilst visiting the area north of Yellowknife we were taken for a drive along the ice roads, (they later featured in British television programme, 'Ice Road Truckers.') Our hosts were hoping to show us a herd of migrating caribou or moose. It was quite an experience to drive along the ice road. The surface continually bowed under the weight of the big four wheel drive vehicles and it all felt very unsafe.

The vehicles were parked by the roadside and we split up to continue our journey on skidoos (snow scooters). Unfortunately we didn't see any sign of the caribou or moose, but as we travelled deep into the forest along frozen paths, I was surprised to see what looked like a fox standing in an icy clearing. We both pointed in that direction and rode towards it. As we got closer the animal appeared to grow larger in size until the fire officer I was riding with, suddenly made an emergency stop. He did this without warning, and we skidded to a sudden halt in a flurry of snow. Unprepared for this, I banged my face on the back of his left shoulder cutting my lip.

I looked up to see what had startled my companion, and to my great surprise I saw that the animal wasn't a fox; it was a very large, silver and grey timber wolf which was standing proudly in the middle of the snowy track that divided two parts of the forest. It was about fifty yards away from where we stopped and was certainly close enough for me to see its powerful shoulder muscles twitching and I knew this was not a good sign.

The wolf weighed about one hundred and eighty pounds, most of it rippling muscle. Standing almost three feet high at the shoulders, it was about five feet long, with its bushy tail held high, arrogantly over its back. The under parts of the body were tan, but its shoulders and neck were cobalt grey. It had a large head with pointed ears and large paws at the end of its long legs.

We found ourselves in a nervous stand-off. We stared at the magnificent creature and it stared confidently back at us with its expressive amber eyes, sniffing the air as it did so. I could feel the tension in the cold still breeze. It didn't seem to be in any way intimidated by us and this made me anxious. There was no one else around and it was very quiet.

We didn't say a word; we just watched one of Mother Nature's secrets unfold. The local Slavee first nation people believed that wolves and men were closely related spiritually, and I could feel a strong connection with this animal. I heard it growl as it narrowed its piercing eyes; it appeared menacing and aggressive and was obviously not going to stand down. I had previously trained police dogs and recognised these canine traits; every sinew appeared poised as though waiting for the instruction to attack. Unarmed, I felt very vulnerable.

I felt powerless in this tense situation because I was on the back of the skidoo and could not reach any of the controls. I could have got off the skidoo but that would have been reckless, and exceptionally dangerous. We didn't speak so I didn't know what was going through my companion's mind. We certainly couldn't try to turn around because that would have left our backs exposed which could have triggered a violent chase.

After what seemed like minutes, although it was more likely to be seconds, the fire officer made a move. He suddenly revved up the engine of the skidoo and rode it straight at the wolf. It happened so quickly that I nearly fell off backwards. As he did this the wolf looked startled, but did not move, he still held his ground. My immediate concern changed. Now it was not for me or my colleague, it was now for the safety of this magnificent animal.

I thought, 'Please run into the woods,' as I didn't want to see it   unnecessarily injured or killed. As we came within twenty five yards, I could see the wolf's muscles tense and ripple. Its expression changed and it turned and slipped away into the undergrowth of the thick pine forest. I'm glad it did, but I'll never forget coming face to face with this kindred spirit.

Aurora Borealis

I was cold and tired, lying in my sleeping bag as the wind buffeted against the thin canvas, but I had been disturbed by a flash of bright light that lit up the tent. There were no inhabitants for at least a hundred miles in any direction so this naturally made me feel apprehensive. Reluctantly I decided to pluck up the courage to get out of my sleeping bag and go outside to find out what had caused this sudden vivid light.

As I nervously unzipped the tent door, I was pleasantly surprised because it was not as cold or as dark outside as I had expected it to be. The wind was only slight, and it had obviously sounded far worse from inside the tent where the thin canvas amplified the noise.

Standing up and stretching my stiff back I looked around in disbelief, and couldn't believe what I saw; it was magical, just like a Hans Christian Andersen fairy story. Bright streaks of green light were lying in the night sky; hanging like giant lime green curtains acting as though they were a window to the universe, or maybe as a portal to the Slavee gods. The unwritten local folklore suggested that the lights are *'manifestations of spirits in the night sky'*. Staring at the gorgeous sky I could understand why they believed this; it certainly felt supernatural.

There was a warm glow around me and I felt reassuringly close to my dad, who had only recently passed away. I could almost hear him saying 'What have you got yourself involved in this time?' I wanted to continue the conversation but didn't know how, and this made me feel sad. All my emotions felt heightened, to the point that I didn't know whether to laugh or cry.

Trying hard to concentrate on what I was looking at, I saw that the exquisite heavenly lights were in a fixed position in the night sky. They also appeared to be wispy and hazy, almost like the fluorescent flames flickering out of a log fire. The beautiful luminous rays flickered in radiant grandeur like a scene from an opulent eighteenth century ballroom. Staring at this ethereal dance I could see several shades of bright yellow, coppery red and even a deep purple tinge, all swirling in amongst the exquisite green gossamer twists.

Looking closer I could see that the vivid green trails of light weren't permanent; they were shimmering and fading. They had a sheen like the surface of crushed velvet drapes. This array contrasted with the black sky beautifully lit up by innumerable bright stars, the odd fast moving satellite, and the stunningly clear and sparkling crescent moon. The pristine white landscape reflected the dancing colours above our heads. I closed my eyes and felt as though I could reach out and touch the plumes of light; they seemed to be so close all around me.

I stood transfixed, enjoying the moment. My knees felt weak and I could feel goose bumps. I wanted to talk but was too emotional to speak, and every sound seemed amplified in the still night. All of my senses were excited. I had never seen the *Aurora Borealis* (The Northern Lights), but had read so much about them. I even bought postcards depicting them, but now they looked dynamic and so different from the photographs.

It was a very atmospheric and emotional experience and to appreciate it you had to be a part of the whole package, to be there both mentally and physically. Strangely it reminded me of scuba diving in the sea, where everything is so quiet and tranquil and all around there is bright green seaweed hanging from the water's surface.

The *Aurora Borealis* is an atmospheric phenomenon which occurs when charged particles are expelled from the sun's surface. This 'solar wind' reacts with the Earth's oxygen and nitrogen atoms in the outer atmosphere and makes the particles glow. The Earth's magnetic field concentrates the solar wind at the magnetic poles, in a similar way to that of iron fillings attracted to the ends of a bar magnet. This is why we see the Aurora only at extreme northern and southern latitudes.

This light show is named after the Roman goddess of dawn, '*Aurora*', and the Greek name for the north wind, '*Borealis*'. People are prepared to travel thousands of miles to see it, but those who live near to the Polar Regions will have witnessed it from the beginning of time. Interestingly there are some North American Inuit who call the *Aurora Borealis* '*aqsarniit*'; they say the lights in the sky are the spirits of the dead playing football with the head of a walrus. The First Nation people of Hudson Bay have a simpler explanation; they call it *'the spirit torches that guide the dead to the land of light that lies beyond the black shell of the sky'*.

The lights have been observed since ancient times, and the first recorded account was from a Babylonian clay tablet from around 568 BC.

I was lost in the moment, staring incredulously at the stunning scenery, and realised that this no longer felt like a dangerous place. It looked beautiful and appeared so peaceful, inviting and serene. Everything was so clear and bright; it no longer felt cold, harsh and unwelcome, and I was very content.

Memories of Felley Woods

I have visited Felley Woods frequently over the last twenty-seven years and wherever I have been in the world my thoughts always return to that beautiful wooded area close to my home in Nottinghamshire.

Memories of the woods have always motivated me when I needed them most. I recollect the sight of the graceful red kites gliding leisurely on the thermals high above the valley near to America's Farm, and the carpets of beautiful bluebells on the forest floor. I think about the old farm buildings, the disused lime kiln, Haggs Farm, the remains of Beauvale Priory and The Old Hunt Kennels, described by DH Lawrence in *'Sons and Lovers'* and *'The White Peacock'*. He called it 'The country of my heart'. This area is also close to the ancestral home of the poet Lord Byron who I imagined walking around the footpaths with his faithful dog Boatswain. These literary thoughts have always inspired me.

I have fond summer memories of walking along the dusty footpaths, through woods of sycamore, birch, oak, and beech; running in the dappled sunlight as the pathways opened out onto the beautiful cornfields, I picture and smell the golden sun-drenched wheat gently swaying in the warm breeze. In springtime, I cycle past the spectacular sea of bluebell and dog's mercury, the Blackthorn bushes in full flower and the bright yellow fields of oil seed rape. My thoughts of autumn are of beautiful copper and pale yellow leaves covering the forest floor; the nights drawing in, and the trees silhouetted against the backdrop of beautiful sunsets. Winter brings pink and purple sunrises, pine trees laden with snow, cold air, and the sight of bare, bony branches of deciduous trees tossing in the heavy winds.

Early one morning in late March, I walked in the woods, it was misty, and damp underfoot. As I left the footpath to stroll in the knotted undergrowth of the trees I could see that the beech, oak and sycamore were not yet in leaf, but the tall scots pines displayed their bottle green pine needles and chestnut brown cones. It felt peaceful in the stillness and I was comfortable surrounded by nature. I could hear the sound of my footsteps as they scrunched through the damp undergrowth and slid over the mossy fallen logs. Listening intently I heard the screeching staccato voices of bird song, then the flutter of unseen wings. The cool breeze rustled through the higher branches of the mature trees.

There had been heavy rain and the small streams had become swollen, the clear water surging and splashing along the muddy banks, carrying with it woody debris. Plumes of foam appeared where the flow was momentarily impeded by rocks. There was a smell of the distinctive bitter-sweet pine needles, tree bark, and the damp forest, as the mist swirled, creating new shadows and dark patches, revealing sudden clear views of my surroundings.

Through the shifting dawn light I saw the lichen on the trees, and the shaded mottled undergrowth. A breeze carried the ripe smell of damp wood and earthy fungus. Suddenly there was a flurry of activity as a large fallen tree branch snapped under my foot, disturbing a family of grey squirrels. Then there was peace and calm once again.

Breaking the silence a large fallow stag deer close by nibbled on the new tasty shoots in the undergrowth. He moved his head up and down and the hot breath steamed from his mouth. As his head moved he revealed his long fawn antlers and I counted twelve points, but one was broken away. His beautiful brown coat, tinged with grey, had a silky sheen, and his muscles rippled along his powerful haunches and sleek torso. The expressive face twitched, as he was disturbed by a noise in the bushes and his great powerful body lurched. Hardly making a sound he faded away into a large glade of birch trees.

The Back of my Head

I didn't realise the back of my head looked like that, having never seen that view before. My hair is wavier than I imagined and I have odd ears, the left one is far bigger than the right. That was something I never knew!

Having always been vain, I was meticulous, and used to enjoy looking in mirrors and never missed an opportunity to view myself in a glass reflection. I liked to brush my full head of black hair, scrupulously shaving my face and rubbing the sleep out of my eyes.

Unfortunately, my world has now been shattered and now all I can see is the back of my head. There is nothing attractive about the back of a head; there are no identifying features, in fact it is boring beyond belief, but at least I don't have to worry about my ever-increasing wrinkles. Staring at this view, I wonder what thoughts are written upon my face, I'm sure it must look sad.

I don't know what I have done to deserve this, not having been a bad person. Okay, I drink and sometimes gamble, but have always tried to treat people with kindness and respect. Eight weeks ago, I remember riding my bike, training for a sponsored event, the next thing I knew I was in hospital having just come out of a coma. The surgeon told me that the front of my head had been damaged beyond repair. Apparently I had been hit from behind by a young, drunk driver; he had been speeding, doing fifty miles an hour in a thirty limit. I hadn't stood a chance. That is all I know about the incident, and certainly don't remember it.

My frontal lobes had been crushed and I am now suffering from a rare form of brain damage. As the result, I can only see the back of my head. The surgeon said that he thought that I would be able to see my face, but my brain cannot cope with the horrific injuries and it is interpreting my vision in a different way. Now it's hard to know what to believe because the view of my back appears real and I can see it move when I turn this way and that.

No one knows what to do with me, surgery is not an option without risking further cranial damage; and psychotherapy is difficult when you can only lie face down on the couch. There are some advantages to my situation though, I am now the best groomed person I know from the back, I wash my neck and behind my ears at least twice every day and there are no long errant hairs sticking out from the back of my ear lobes. Now I don't need anyone's help, because I can watch my own back!

The Earth's Shadow

The arctic dusk slowly descended and I watched as the sun dipped towards the horizon. I didn't realise it, but I was about to witness a precious life experience that I would never forget.

Owing to the spectacular enormity of what was happening around me I stopped, and stood transfixed, watching the dusky sky change dramatically before me. It was a great surprise, and I felt privileged to watch the beauty of what was unfolding.

The majestic flaming sun went from pale yellow to bright red and then to an intense scarlet, growing fatter as it sank like a tumbling red beach ball into the horizon. It was as though it was reluctant to disappear from view. Darkness descended and everything was crystal clear, with no light pollution for hundreds of miles in any direction.

I watched as the sun set in the west, and half the sky turned a beautiful rich crimson and burgundy, the shade of which I had only ever seen in a narrow strip of rainbow. As the twilight deepened I was aware of something happening in the opposite direction. I looked east and saw a dark band of magnificent deep violet rising above the horizon, I had never seen this stunningly beautiful colour before. and was excited.

This spectacular violet shade found in the eastern sky, is called the 'Earth's Shadow.' It occurs where the Earth casts its shadow from the sun's rays onto its own atmosphere, and always appears on the opposite side to the sunset. It can best be seen near to the Earth's geographic poles in exceptionally clear conditions where there is a long uninterrupted horizon.

I felt a tingling down my spine, and goosebumps, and momentarily lost my breath, but knew this pulsating sensation was not caused by the extreme cold, as I could also feel a warm glow on my skin. Elated, I realised that this was not just a visual experience it was also an intensely emotional one. Feeling like I could laugh and cry at the same time, it was like re-living my whole life in just a few intense seconds. My legs felt like jelly, and I almost lost balance on the ice.

I could not believe the magnificence of what I saw. I felt special and had to pinch myself to check that I was still awake. I came to the conclusion that if this is what heaven is like then we have nothing to fear! Lost in time, my very being was overcome by this precious moment.

The phenomenon must have lasted for about five minutes, then seemed to be over almost as soon as it had begun. Suddenly, just like a camera flash, the shining ice below the sun seemed to come alive with the reflection of a rich splash of colour, almost as if an artist had just thrown the remains of his palette onto the sparkling white canvas.

As the setting sun reluctantly disappeared from view the remarkable colours slowly began to fade into darkness. Then as if at a pre-ordained signal, the stars lit up the night sky like a cascade of sparkling diamonds, each with its own infinitesimal myriad of beautiful shimmering colours. I was surprised because these had not been evident before, and neither had the bright crescent-shaped moon, which seemed to glow like a beacon guiding our lonely path in the darkened night sky.

I hadn't realised, but my colleagues had also slowed down to watch the unfolding scene. My head was still full of this beautiful imagery as we began to ski, following Mike in orderly single file. I felt full of life, enthusiastic, with renewed energy. The gods were watching over us and guiding our route into the unknown. I felt at one with my surroundings, and the universe.

Alfred Holt

Born and raised in South London, I now live in Pinxton having retired five years ago. Before that, I trained and worked as a chef for twenty-four years. I started writing four years ago, and tend to write romantic poetry and light hearted short stories.

A member of Jacksdale Jotters, and the Eastwood Writers Group, I have been published in some local newspapers and magazines.

Acrostic Rose

My Rose, with a figure so slender
Is a queen of love in every way.
Kisses applied with lips so tender,
Every morning, and at close of day.
Shining eyes, red lips and golden hair;
Crowned in glory brightens all my life
And my sweet best beloved one will share
Red roses when at last you are my wife.
I will in awe stand when I see you there,
Shall we stem the currents of desire?
Atone for wrongs, or have no care,
Forgetting not the calling that is higher?
As long as I am able, dearest mate,
Never will my passion ebb like tide,
Nor will we ever let our love abate.
You are my life and always by my side,
My soul so blessed shall never dark despair,
Always the rose with breakfast shall I serve,
Giving and taking freely with such care,
Near the end our memories we reserve.
Enamoured of the life so richly shared.
The red rose, you and I, no longer there.

A life not lived

Is our only life foretold and drawn
In Heaven's book?
Are we yoked as blindfold oxen
Treading to the master's whim?
If somehow we returned to see
What might and might not be
Could we then be free of him?
I think not, what's done is done,
Predestined, as blind men shuffle
With guiding hand on shoulder,
 "This way – come".
Kindness fleeting, not for all,
Perhaps for some who love life
And whom life loves back.
For others just the lonely road
To blessed oblivion's silent hall.
Some welcome death's slow tread upon the stair,
Their face alight with joy when life departs.
Cowardly or bold, it nought avails
When shutters softly close at last, who cares?

That Day

On that day when the weather was fine,
The Reaper walked the Great Western Line.
His head was high and his scythe was bright,
His job was to last well into the night.

Clackety-clack sent some off to sleep,
Their secrets now forever to keep.
All hope gone, only shadows in fright,
This will surely be Lucifer's night.

With papers and books, few chose to read,
No time to review their personal creed.
Lulled by the train, unaware of their fate,
With death and destruction lying in wait.

Dead man's handle in the driver's hand,
The train sped swiftly across the land.
All sitting safely on comfy seats,
Children sucking on sticky treats.

Wild wind was keening a deathly wail,
Engine bound to the guiding rail,
Black smoke streaming, an unkempt mane,
While carriages creaked and couplings strained.

The red light warning passed unseen,
As the Devil's hand uncovered the green.
The train went on to meet another;
Death to baby, father and mother.

His job was done and all lay dead,
No-one that night would see their bed.
The Devil he leaped and danced away,
Content with his work upon that day.

The Journey

Our journey started in our prime;
We listened to the church bells' chime,
With promise of a lovely life,
T'was then I took you for my wife.

It was amidst those August days,
So happy in our joyful ways,
Also blessed with golden weather,
We knew we would grow old together.

Under the stars of moonlit nights,
Embracing in our own delights,
So young and free, our cares so few,
I was so glad I married you.

We journeyed all life's bumpy roads,
And had to carry many loads,
But together we found a way,
To help us through each taxing day.

We travelled on just me and you,
When we were blessed with another two.
Years passed before they flew the nest,
Time then, my love, to have a rest.

But time flows on, as Nature shows,
And every life fades, like the rose.
Alas, arrived that dreadful day
When you, my wife, did slip away.

I was then well past my prime,
Alone to hear the church bell chime.
With journey's ending of our life,
I'm glad I took you for my wife.

The Ticking Bomb

Mildred looked at the telegram for the millionth time. She placed it on her bedside table, and walked to his side of the bed staring intensely, as if to see him there. She stooped, placed her hands on her knees, lowered her head, and kissed the pillow fervently. Tears soaked the spot where her dearest Robert once lay.

The sirens sounded, she heard neighbours running. "Come on Millie, there's a dud stuck in Robson Street. It's ticking!" shouted a familiar but perturbed voice through her letterbox. However, she stayed with the pillow; transfixed to where her lover had once slept.

Mildred had heard the woman, and somewhere in her heart she knew the siren was calling her to safety. Nevertheless, she did feel safe. Her whole being was secure in the knowledge she could soon be with her beloved Robert. She shouted back at the woman, "Be down in a minute, Rube." Then, reluctantly, she pulled herself away and walked to the living room, swigged some brandy from the bottle on the mantelpiece, went back to the bedroom and lay on the bed cuddling the pillow.

Outside, Bobbies were running around clearing the streets; shouting through megaphones and banging on doors until silence fell on the deserted, doomed street.

Minutes later there was an almighty 'BANG!', and bits of once-cherished homes showered the area.

As Mildred had promised herself, she and Robert were now together.

Pat Lowe

Blessed with a wonderful family, great friends, and the guidance of angels, I began a misspent youth selling handbags on Blackpool promenade. I then moved on to the challenges of educating young minds. Creative writing suits my tendency never to let the truth get in the way of a good story!

Machu Picchu

Turning three hundred and sixty degrees, I stare up at the blistering cloudless sky. The morning mists have cleared to reveal sharp pointed mountains painted deep forest green, surrounding us.

I draw in a deep lungful of the clean crystal air as the overpowering beauty of this mysterious, majestic place floods my senses.

Where was everyone? Two thousand five hundred tourists invade this sacred city every day in convoys of dusty buses which slowly snake up the mountain like ants, from the village of Aguas Calientes below.

Today there is almost no-one, only a few stragglers who came with me from the village and walkers coming in from the Sun Gate after walking the Inca trail, their huge back packs and equipment obliterating the tiny Sherpas who carried them.

The buses stand empty and silent and this beautiful magical Machu Picchu in Peru, built on top of the world, twelve thousand feet above sea level, is deserted and all mine.

I meander over the steep terraced hillside which was built to keep invaders out of this lost city of the Incas. The sun-bleached dry stone walls are packed so tightly together that not even a leaf could be put between them; so skilled were the craftsmen.

Two beautiful white butterflies shiver, flutter and dance with each other around my head. They play, kiss and gossip, keeping their secrets of this special spiritual place; it touches me very deeply.

Hidden for over five hundred years, and with many whisperings down the vista of time, it wasn't discovered until 1911. It is a religious site built in 1450 amidst the surrounding sacred mountains, and was never found by the Spanish.

I sit down heavily on the stone steps as altitude sickness suddenly engulfs me with a wave of nausea. A native Peruvian guide in colourful costume wanders over and gives me some coca leaves to chew on. He has a flattened nose and large nostrils as all Peruvians have, so as to take in more oxygen. His face is reddened, not by the sun, but by capillaries close to the surface of his skin. The leaves do the trick, and I feel much better, but it isn't until much later that I discover they are the leaves from which cocaine is made.

Hour after hour I wander over this sacred land, through buildings with sophisticated water channels fed from natural springs, enjoying the stillness, the peace, the oneness with nature, all the time wondering where the other tourists are?

The city was allegedly built for the virgins of the sun, who made offerings of food to the Sun God, and indeed there was enough land to grow food for four times the city population. But why did this strange and mysterious place disappear for centuries of time? Where did all the lost souls go before the undergrowth twisted and strangled the life from the city? Nobody knows.

Eventually, as the silent sun is sinking, I trundle down the mountain in the bus and back to the village where I am staying another night. Only whilst in a local café eating the national dish of guinea pig do I find out that all the trains bringing in the daily tourists from Cusco, fifty miles away, are on strike. Only the people staying in the village, as I am, could make it up the mountain.

How lucky am I?

My Track

Down the dusty track
Under a cloudless sky
A thousand shades of green
In a moment catch my eye

A wedding veil of cow parsley
A swishing wave of wheat
Buzzards faintly mewling
Under the blistering heat

Cabbage whites and dragonflies
Caressed by late August sun
Full-blooded blackberries ripening
Now summer's nearly done

O Sole Mio

It was quiet, the last week in October, and the end of the season. The scarlet hibiscus was still in flower as were the bubbles of purple bougainvillea which blazed in a shimmering haze. Patrisco was clearing the tables as the last of the summer visitors wound their way off the beach.

He loved the calm and the peace after the frantic rush of summer. It was cooler, quiet, just perfect. The sun sparkled on the sea like a thousand diamonds as he wondered if he ought to leave it a few more days before he called an end to the season. Although the café was closing for winter, he still had a job in the evenings as a singer in the local hotels. As a classically trained tenor, it was a job he loved. Not that everyone appreciated the classics.

Patrisco got to sing all his favourite songs, and with his dark Italian looks, broken English, and teeth as white as piano keys, he'd had his fair share of girls who loved to be serenaded. Nearing thirty, he'd no responsibility, no commitment and romance only lasted a fortnight at the most. Which was how he liked it. His was the best job in the world. He lived his life in paradise, on his little island of Minorca whose lush green landscape with rocky inlets and private bays nourished his soul.

He was cleaning the inside of the ice cream machine when he first noticed her. Alone and beautiful she walked off the beach, her long blond hair matching the yellow sarong which caressed the voluptuous curves of her body. She carried herself with confidence, completely comfortable in her own skin.

Hose pipe in hand, he stood and watched her all the

way to the hire car, staring as she drove off, a vision of beauty heading towards Mahon. Giving thanks for the pleasant interlude, he hurriedly finished the cleaning as he had a performance in El Castille on the other side of the island that evening.

On stage, staring into a field of faces, he gave a perfect rendition of 'Empty chairs at empty tables' from *Les Miserables*. The audience cheered for more and in his Italian accent he thanked them and promised one more song.

It was then Patrisco noticed the girl again walking towards the bar, her long pony tail swinging. He was positive it was her. He'd recognise that walk anywhere, and just as an artist appreciates beauty, so did he.

When he finished, to rapturous applause, he made his way to the bar but she'd disappeared. Well, at least he knew which hotel she was staying in. He thought it was quite strange to see her again but was looking forward to relaxing on his day off.

The following morning promised to be heavenly. Patrisco headed to his favourite café in Fornelles where he could drink coffee outside and watch the boats in the harbour, nodding and bowing in the wind. He loved listening to the tinkling of the masts like giant wind chimes, and letting the sun energise him. He had just taken his second sip, when, with arm still raised he spotted the girl again heading for the café, a book under her arm. Patrisco followed her every move from behind his designer sunglasses. What a coincidence, but then in his eyes there was no coincidence.

Sitting a few tables away he heard her order a cappuccino. It took seconds to decide what to do. Leaving his coffee behind he walked over and with his best smile and in broken English he asked her if she'd enjoyed his singing. Blinking frantically with her long luscious lashes, desperately trying to remember him, she stared helplessly until it finally dawned on her that he was the tenor from the previous night.

She asked him to join her and said her name was Charlotte. He told her he'd seen her twice the previous day. He told her about his family who were still living in Sorrento and how he'd lived on the island for ten years.

She explained that she'd walked away from a messy divorce with no children and was free and single again. They shared a love of books and theatre and by the end of the week he knew he'd met the girl of his dreams. They made plans to meet her parents in England and although he didn't want to admit it, he had fallen deeply in love with her. The nights they spent together in the flat above the café were the best nights of his life. This was no holiday 'fling', and his heart sang with a joy that was reflected in his performances to the delighted audiences who flocked to hear him.

On her last evening he'd invited her to the San Bou hotel where he was giving his final performance of the season. There was a capacity crowd, and the place hummed with expectation.

Patrisco sat on a stool and nodded to the barman, who passed him a glass of mineral water. Reaching into his pocket, Patrisco pulled out his mobile phone and dialled his mother's number. She would be so glad he was coming home, and he had so much to tell her. He got through and at once heard his mother's voice " Eyup, Pat! Nice t' hear from thee son. When are t'coming 'ome?"

"Eyup mam" said Patrisco, "Art owreet? Eeh by 'eck it'll be grand to see thee. Bin a long season this year, and

I'm reet ready forra break. I've a lot ta tell thee, and some gradely news!"

Patrisco's mum babbled away from distant Yorkshire, but he didn't hear what she said, as suddenly he looked up at the mirror behind the bar. Behind him he saw Charlotte, eyes wide with dismay, face white with shock. He turned, dropping the phone, which squeaked tinnily on the bar top.

Too late. She fled from the hotel and disappeared into the night. As he burst through the front door of the hotel, heart pounding and suffused with a feeling of sick dread, he saw her driven away in a taxi.

That night, his performance was spellbinding, and many of the women in the audience were moved to tears as he sang the heartbreaking operatic arias. Many who heard him remarked on the fact that he sang with real feeling, and how the ladies swooned at that beautiful Italian accent.

The Cucumber Sandwich

It was calm and quiet and there was a heavy, damp grey stillness which hung in the spring air. The winter's beech tree leaves still clung to its sleeping body like crispy toast. Snowdrops with their baby's eyes peeped out from under the awakening earth.

A slight stirring shivered the leaves which trembled gently in the breeze. The whole hedge started shaking, which was very odd, as the rest of the garden was perfectly still. Not a daffodil nodded, nor a crocus swayed, only the angry dancing of the beech hedge.

And then I saw it! Very, very, slowly, almost too slowly to notice, the leaves began to change their colour. They went from burnt brown to a very pale blue. From the very tips, this pale blue 'blood' flowed right through their veins, covering every crevice, becoming darker and darker as it wandered on its course along the hedge.

What on earth was happening? I looked around. Every other plant and flower was perfectly normal. Nothing else had changed, except for the shaking, angry, now royal blue beech hedge. A silver glint caught my eye, moving from side to side in the mass of blue. It appeared to be a small light, flickering as it dipped in and out of the leaves.

With eyes strained I could just make out what seemed to be a wing trapped amongst the branches; a very angry insect fighting to free itself. I ran downstairs and out of the front door, desperate to see what was happening. I hadn't been dreaming. There it was. Something bright blue in the hedge. But it wasn't a trapped insect. This was a tangled, tousled, fairy. A fairy with attitude!

Not only did the hedge turn blue, but the air as well, as she stamped, swore, and cursed as she tried to free herself.

"I'll help you," I yelled.

"No you blinkin' well won't," she spat.

I dived in and gently grasped her tiny body which fitted neatly into the palm of my hand. It felt deliciously warm! I had just untangled the gossamer wing made of tiny cobweb strands, when I felt a sharp pain. The little minx had bitten my finger! I opened my palm and she flew up into the sky, sticking her tongue out at me on the way up. I blinked, and she had gone. I turned round and the hedge had returned to its normal colour. The breeze had died away.

Had I imagined all this? I walked inside, made a cucumber sandwich, and then as I buttered the bread, a bright red drop appeared, spreading across the crust, dripping from the end of my finger; just where she had bitten me!

The Weekend Man

Her short arm couldn't quite reach the ticket from the toll machine, and every weekend she had to undo the seatbelt or risk scraping the wing mirror. Smiling inwardly she laughed to herself, after all it was a small price to pay.

Driving up the hillside near Alcoy, Alicia found herself desperate for the loo. Pulling into what she thought was a café on her way to meet a friend at Patrico, who had a new baby, she pushed open the heavy wooden door.

'No, we are a shop,' said a voice through beautiful pearly teeth , 'selling marmalade my brother makes in his factory next door.'

Alicia scanned his olive skin and unusual blue eyes, which seemed to twinkle with every emotion. Instantly forgetting her need for the loo, and enquiring about the jams and chutneys, she fell into an animated conversation with this appealing stranger, who went out of his way to tell her he was an artist.

'My mother lived in Tenerife and I studied art at university there. I also teach in my spare time, a little sculpture too.' He grinned, his floppy fringe lending him a youthful air, full of vitality.

'Could I see one of your paintings?' she asked innocently.

'Of course, I'm working on one at the moment in the garden'.

She followed him outside and around the back. It was February, and turning the corner she stopped to marvel at a vision of pink organza; the almond trees were in full bloom.

A painting propped up on an easel took her breath away. A simple view of the garden, with the masses of blossom everywhere, it was a celebration of life and vibrant colour.

'It's beautiful, may I buy it?'

'It's not finished yet, it will be at least another hour.'

So, sitting on a chair next to him and chatting as he worked, Alicia listened to his hopes and dreams of how he was going to sell his paintings in the restaurant he would build next to the marmalade factory. In all this time he'd had no other customers.

'As you can see, I have plenty of time for painting. It's not often I have someone as beautiful and intelligent as you to talk to.'

She wanted to be more than friends, and hoped he might ask her out. He didn't say anything. Maybe he didn't like her enough?

He, on the other hand didn't want to appear too forward, and scare her away. She knew his location should she wish to visit. He would leave it at that.

They dragged out the time, lingering desperately until it was awkward to stay any longer. The painting was finished hours ago.

'How much do I owe you?'

'Nothing, it's a gift, with my compliments'.

He carried it to her car, trying to explain complicated instructions of how to dry the oils. They fleetingly brushed fingers as she arranged it in the boot. Eyes lingered, smiles held unspoken desire. Why doesn't he ask me out? she wondered. With a heavy heart she got into the car, said her goodbyes and drove off.

Her friend was well. Alicia couldn't properly concentrate; she oohed and aahed over the new baby until a decent length of time had passed and she could take her leave without seeming churlish.

Pulling into his car park on the way back she saw the shop was closed. So much for wanting to find out his intentions. Now she would never know.

Over the years throughout her marriage, he still crept into her thoughts and dreams; daytime, night-time. She could remember every word, every smile and twinkle, never ageing. The painting took pride of place. Many times her husband and children wanted it thrown away, said it was old fashioned and dated. They liked new modern paintings.

She grew busier; the years crept by, but inside her loneliness grew. 'The man from the shop' was her soul mate, she knew, and eventually after twenty years, Alicia decided she would bury her restless demons. Would the shop still be there? Would he still be there?

February again, and the friend's daughter had delivered a baby. A perfect excuse to visit. With shaking hands she opened the shop door. A middle- aged woman, her eye on two young children, smiled at her pleasantly.

'Can I help you?'

The building had changed. It was now a restaurant with an adjoining door through which Alicia could see diners enjoying their meals.

'Just looking. How long have you been here?'

'Ten years. This is my husband's. He's supposed to be helping with the meals'.

A shrill bell suddenly rang.

'Excuse me, I will be back,' she said, smiling as she disappeared through the door.

Alone, Alicia surveyed the shop. Still basically the same, but now littered with paintings on every wall, a still life propped up against dusty shelves. She wandered around the back to find the almond trees blazing with life. She held a waxy blossom in her hand, smelt its perfumed fragrance. A small breeze caught the leaves, wafted the petals over her like confetti at a wedding.

In the far corner a small wooden easel was tucked away, a paintbrush working vigorously. Walking up nervously she said brightly 'Hola, do you remember me?'

He turned, a small frown disappearing from his forehead, 'How could I forget that smile?'His hair, much greyer now, was still thick, and flopped over his eyes as it always did. Apart from a few wrinkles he was exactly the same. So many questions, so little time.

'Why did you not visit me, why has it taken you so long?' He nibbled the end of his brush and fixed her with those piercing eyes.

'I thought you weren't interested.' She sounded petulant and looked away.

'How wrong you were, and still are. Nobody has occupied my dreams more than you -- now it's too late. I am married, so are you.' He glared at her ring.

'I can't let you go again. Meet me somewhere private. We need to talk.'

So an apartment was bought in Benidorm. Alicia drove from Valencia every weekend using the pretext of watching her friend's baby grow up; and every weekend she struggled with the toll machine. He was her weekend man, and she loved it.

133

White Peonies

White peonies why are you sad

in the full bloom of life?

Why do you surrender to summer storms,

battered and bruised, frilly skirts lying helpless?

So slow to bloom

So quick to die.

Huge creamy meringues drooping,

dissolving in the wretched rain.

Stretching your necks like dying swans,

teardrops falling until you are gone.

Shirley McIntyre

I've always fancied myself as a wordsmith, but since retiring I've been able to focus more on my writing. I'm proud of my very modest successes which include a regular column in a local newspaper! Thanks to everyone who encourages, critiques and enjoys my jottings - but thanks most of all to Dolly and BoBo, and Jake and Jenny Blackbird, who inspire so many of my musings.

Boggle Hole

"If I see another fusty fossil, I swear I'll die," said Sue, peering in the mirror of her powder compact.

There we were, twenty-five young teenage girls shivering and complaining in 'Boggle Hole', a youth hostel in Fylingthorpe, just outside Robin Hoods Bay, North Yorkshire. This was day three of our Easter field trip, and it had yet to stop raining.

We were all missing our warm, comfy beds, but for Sue, the Prima Donna of 3A1, the constant foraging for fossils and seaweed was just too much. She *was* a sight. The Yorkshire frets had transformed her normally luxurious curls, into a ball of yellow frizz, her nose was red and flaky as we'd all caught colds, and the mascara she painstakingly applied each morning had run and dried into sooty salty streams on her cheeks. Poor Sue was feeling the deprivations of 'roughing it' more than the rest of us.

The trip had begun well. Mr Fisher - Geography, and Miss Goldsmith - Science, even joined in our singing, and the rickety bus rocked to the sounds of the sixties. Our eyes were like saucers, when stuffy, old-fashioned Miss Goldsmith said,

'Actually, I went to school with Brian Poole.'

'Not THE Brian Poole. Not Brian Poole of the Tremeloes?' We shrieked in disbelief.

Miss Goldsmith just nodded and smiled, so the rest of the journey was devoted to an impromptu medley of 'Here Comes My Baby' 'Even The Bad Times Are Good' and 'Do You Love Me?'

Later, in the stark dormitory, I looked on enviously as Sue unpacked her shiny patent suitcase. Whilst my scruffy duffle bag spewed out a motley collection of hand-me-downs, it was clear that Sue's mum had spent a fortune on designer clothes from the latest 'mod' boutiques springing up around Nottingham.

We both had the requisite trousers and sweaters, but any similarity to our respective holiday gear ended there. When I spotted my friend's lemon negligee lounging on the top bunk, I hurriedly shoved my knobbly dressing gown, with its fraying tasselled belt, back in my bag.

Every day followed a similar pattern, scavenging on the rainy beach each morning, and then drawing and writing about our briny finds in the chilly Boggle Hole classroom. We never completely dried out.

On the last day we went to Hull. It was like being out on parole. We all got tarted up. Miss Goldsmith and Mr Fisher were engrossed in taking photos of each other in the harbour, so we were left to our own devices. For me and Sue, this included being chatted up by some Yorkshire lads, who offered us a Park Drive Tipped, We took turns puffing on this illicit ciggie, with all the sophistication of a seasoned smoker, flicking ash nonchalantly hither and thither.

Finally we were going home, on the rickety bus heading for Nottingham. We were scruffy, smelly, tired and cold. A few die-hards attempted a maudlin rendition of Roy Orbison's 'It's Over', but nobody was in the mood for singing.

At school on Monday when we were refreshed by hot baths, own beds, and decent food, our week of deprivation quickly became 'the best five days of our lives'. We made sure we were the envy of the poor unfortunates who'd been unable to go.

Charity bags

I'm fed up with staring at tired old clothes,
That show off my wobbly fat tum.
Shirts with popped buttons, tight jeans with bust zips,
They'll never squash over my bum.

I've got coats that won't shut, and ganzies that gape,
Bras bullied by big bulging breasts.
Despite my best efforts, there's no way my boobs
Will squeeze into tight tiny vests.

So into the charity bag they must go,
'cos I'm sick of the guilt that they bring.
When I look at their shape, and then down at mine,
I know I can't wear things that cling.

Those days are long gone and I have to accept,
I've doubled my young fighting weight.
I'm not a 'petite' (well only in height),
Reminisce about being size eight.

I watch what I eat, take my dogs for long walks,
And generally try to keep healthy.
But no matter what, the pounds just pile on,
They're devious, sneaky and stealthy.

It's out of my hands, this problem with weight,
Need to put it right out of my head.
Accept what I am; wear voluminous clothes,
That camouflage middle age spread.

Dolly's Deliberations

I was six weeks old when I was adopted. I stole Shirley's heart by sitting in the background while my brothers squeaked, tiddled and pooed, clearly oblivious to the enormity of the moment. Gazing at her adoringly, I sidled over to nuzzle her foot. It was a no-brainer.

"This is the one," she cooed, scooping me up. *Back of the net*, I congratulated myself.

After much oohing and aahing, she put me down so I hot-pawed it to the puppy pad and squatted in relief. Phew! Still it was worth it. No gain without pain as they say. I'm sorry to report that my birth mother, Dorothy, seemed unnaturally eager to rid herself of me, her first born. I'm sure I heard her growl, "One down, three to go. Pesky parasitic pups," as she winced at her throbbing, swollen nipples.

When Shirley and Lucy – seemingly my auntie – collected me one October night they said I had another hurdle to jump – Rob, my new Dad. They explained that he might take some getting used to. He'd made it clear he didn't want a dog and had played no part in any puppy preparations. Rob was upstairs feigning disinterest when we arrived.

"Come and meet her Dad," Lucy called. This new scary 'dad' came down, whistling nonchalantly and didn't even give me a glance. "Stroke her then," Auntie urged. Although I was dying for a puppy pad, my nose was dry with anxiety, and my nervous flatulence grumbled ominously, I realised this could be make or break time. So, clenching my bladder and sphincter muscles, I licked his hand then performed the same 'pleading eye' trick that had been Shirley's undoing. It worked. I was home.

Me and Auntie - a sucker for anything with four legs - snuggled up together on the sofa while Shirley and Rob looked online about rearing puppies. *Hmm A bit late in the day for that methinks!!* I was just luxuriating in a tum-tickling session when Lucy shrieked, "Ooh, look at this! I think she's a boy." She pointed to my nether regions, and Mum and Dad peered my bits.

"That does look like a little willie," said Dad. I let out a plaintive squeak in protest and was horrified to hear Shirley say:

"Well I really didn't want a boy, I definitely want a girl. There's been a mistake. Let's see if they'll swap it." What followed was a long embarrassing discussion on the geography and shape of my bits.

"I know," said Lucy, "let's google it. How do you spell genitalia?" Then to my absolute mortification, they compared *my* tuppence to rude pictures on the laptop. After close scrutiny, they agreed finally that I was, after all, female. Now, when I get into bother with Shirley for being naughty, I'm tempted to say, "Is there any wonder I've gone off the rails after you nearly rejected me when you thought I was a boy? I'm bound to have a big greasy chip on my shoulder. Call yourself a mother?" I keep schtum though; there's more than one way to skin a cat, (or dog for that matter)…

I was about three when things changed at McIntyre Mansions. Suddenly Dad was there every day, and I kept hearing the word 'retired'. I think, translated, that meant, 'Dolly - Gets - Longer – Walks.' My Mum was a self-confessed fair-weather walker, so when it rained, she only took me out for my toilet. Now with Dad it was different. He pressed a button on his huge black umbrella, and we strolled along for ages. I didn't mind getting wet, Dad was sheltered under his magical umbrella, and Mum, well, she was happy, dry, and warm with Jeremy Kyle (bleugh!).

So life was pretty good but then Mum got poorly, so I had *two* walks each day. Occasionally, Mum had to stay somewhere called 'a hospital.' Oh I missed her, naturally, but I relished this special time, just Dad and me. To be perfectly truthful, I almost forgot about her after a couple of days. As well as the walks, Dad and I enjoyed plenty of real grub. Not that dried crap Mum insists is full of things called 'nutrients' and 'vitamins', but real grub - burgers, meatballs and kebabs. Then she came home and things changed again. This time though it was serious stuff – BoBo!

That morning, 22nd July 2011, is etched in my memory forever. Dad went upstairs with Mum's tea, and I followed for my morning snuggle, then Dad asked, as usual,

"How are you feeling Shirl?"

"I'm OK," Mum sighed, and then, "Rob, do you know what would really cheer me up?"

"What?" Dad asked anxiously.

"Well, you know how much I love Dolly, don't you?"

"Yeees," he replied, then, "Shirl, what have I said a million times before? No more dogs."

"But Rob you know I can't go on long walks now, and I'm really missing that. Something like a little Shih Tzu doesn't need much exercise and it would get me out in the fresh air." My treacherous mother even managed to seem paler and more breathless than usual as she added, "It'd be company for me while I watch Jeremy, too." I tried my hardest to make Dad understand my thoughts. *Don't do it Dad, you'll only regret it.* Instead he said,

"OK then, you can have one, but not a pup. No more pooing and tiddling inside. I'm not having that. But if it'll make you feel better, well..."

I watched, disgustedly, as Mum scoured sites for Shih Tzus. I pawed her arm, and looked at her and performed the pleading eyes trick but it was all in vain and I was gobsmacked to hear her say, "Don't worry Dolls, I'll soon find you a brother or sister!"

After about an hour she shouted. "I've found one Rob, come and see. He's three, just like Dolly, and he only lives in Nottingham. It's like he's meant just for me!" Dad and I trudged upstairs and looked at a thumbnail of a fluffy little dog - dressed as Father Christmas!

Oh. My. God. Could it get any worse? What a wuss, in fancy dress. Worse than that though he was, without a doubt, fluffy...the fluffiest lapdog you've ever seen. Mum's told me off many, many times for what she calls my prejudice but I simply cannot help it. I Hate Fluffy Lapdogs. No matter how many smacks I get, or how friendly it is. If I meet a fluffy hairball disguised as a dog I just go for it. I probably need anger management, and now they were thinking of adopting one!

"What's its name then – I can't see without my glasses?" Dad squinted at the laptop.

"BoBo," giggled Mu.

"BoBo? What sort of a blooming name is BoBo?"

"Well, that doesn't matter. What's in a name? We'll call him just what you want, duck."
142

"You'd better ring then, you seem set on it."

"Aw, thanks Rob, and if he's not available, there's plenty more - probably won't be black though." *Well, let's pray for that then.* An hour later, just as me and Dad were sweating hairnets digging up spuds, there was a shout,

"Rob, he's still there, we can meet him on Sunday."

"OK," Dad sighed, and rubbed my ears understandingly. I cannot deny it, that feeling of Dad and me, together, in the face of adversity, warmed the cockles of my heart.

Sunday, possibly the worst day of my entire life, arrived all too soon. I couldn't go with them to meet this interloper as I hate cars. Almost but not quite as much as I hate black dogs. Without a doubt I'd have squealed throughout the entire journey. By late afternoon the THREE of them were back. It was happening. The world as I'd known it had disappeared. This was more than confirmed as my duplicitous dad shouted,

"Come on Doll, come and meet BoBo." I skulked across the grass; my normally majestic tail drooped dejectedly between my legs. Disappointment in my 'loving' parents affected me deeply. I'd lost my mojo. Daft, dopey BoBo scampered round *my* garden like it was his own; he poo'd and tiddled in *my* toilet and then, while Mum sipped her Merlot, he jumped on her knee! It was all too much. I went to bed.

When my tummy rumbled I couldn't resist investigating what was on tonight's menu. Mmm, Surf and Turf, my absolute fave. Ok, Ok, I know it's only gristle from their Sunday roast, and Aldi's Flaked Tuna in Brine, but I dribbled in anticipation, almost forgetting BoBo. Not for long though. Dad put out separate bowls and the greedy, cheeky, son-of-a-bitch, sniffed at both, then growled when I attempted to eat from either!

Eventually the little Shih decided on his preferred choice, and stuffed it down his scrawny throat. I'm normally a slow eater, but I needed to keep a weather eye on him, he wasn't getting any of my dinner. My attempts to keep him from my grub brought on my flatulence, and I'm ashamed to admit it but the bottom-burps later were quite unacceptable. Even to me.

I had to share *my* kitchen with BoBo, but he just slept and snored - like he'd been here forever actually. Next morning Dad came down to make tea, and I hot-pawed it upstairs for my morning cuddle with Mum. As she stroked my beautiful velvetine tabs she cooed,

"Morning Dolls." When Dad came in with that dog, and put it on our bed, I almost wept. Then this new hateful brother actually elbowed me away from *my* Mum!

"Hello BoBo," Mum said. "Did you sleep okay?" He wagged his show-off frondy tail and nudged me even harder. "No, BoBo,", Mum, placed him firmly at the end of our bed and I was pathetically grateful for this small gesture. It wasn't long though before he inched his way forward and elbowed me again. When BoBo licked my pathetic mother's hand she was sunk - hopeless!

Talking about tails though, I must recount this little gem. Since BoBo's arrival I've noticed that my tail seems to find its way between my back legs more and more; it hardly ever curls proudly like before, pre-BoBo. This problem was not helped by a conversation I overheard while I was squirrel-watching. Mum and Dad were outside the summer house and BoBo was sprawled out in the sun:

"Rob, have you noticed Dolly's tail?"

"Yes, it's been like that more or less since BoBo

arrived."

"Oh dear, poor, poor Dolly." My mother gushed, and I looked at her gratefully, until she said,

"Hey Rob. I know what's up with her. She's so traumatised by BoBo's arrival, she's got Erectail Dysfunction!"

I'll never forgive her as she kept repeating it between sips of Merlot, "Erectail Dysfunction. Heheheheh. That's a beaut, Erectail Dysfunction..."

Good Intentions

Another day in tramps' land, I wake with throbbing head.
I've no idea just what I've seen, or done, or thought, or
said.
Yesterday's a mystery; each morning it's a daze,
My memory of the night before lost in a rum-soaked
haze.

Today's the start of my new life, another solemn vow,
I'll get a grip, forget the past and concentrate on now.
It's the future that's important, forget the tragedy,
That brought me to this sorry state, the drink's no
remedy.

The hangover is lifting; my head feels like its mine!
Can life be worthwhile again? With you it was just fine.
Our home's still there, it beckons me to take up tenancy.
I've money, car, etcetera; no need for vagrancy.

My sober days are there you see, in terms of grand
possessions,
And maybe if I pulled some strings I'd return to my
profession.
My disappearance I'd just blag, 'I had to get away,'
To lick my wounds and wallow, and sometimes even
pray.

Would I could turn the clock back, put time in reverse
gear,
But I accept that life has gone; my new one starts right
here.
I'm going home, this can't go on, I need stability
As good and upright citizen, of being, well, just me.

I ponder on this pledge of mine, this firm new resolution,
I'll start today this life's no good but I need a solution
To the problem now of coping, without you by my side;
You knew how much you meant to me, and then you went and died.

Familiar tears fall from my eyes with bittersweet remembrance,
As I recall so clearly- your taste - so you - your fragrance.
We were wonderful together, just lovers? No, much more,
I try hard to forget you but the hurt is still too raw.

I missed you so much and still do, I need the panacea,
That drink provides to block the pain, the hurt and nagging fear.
It's 5 o'clock; the day has passed the ache's still sharp and tender,
It's easy now to understand how I went on that first bender.

I need a crutch to help me, after all what's just one drink?
Another slurp, well that's OK to have a quiet think,
About what is the best approach to start my life anew.
I don't know where to start. Oh well, perhaps another few?

Mrs Barratt

Tap, tap, tap, there she was, Mrs Barratt. To me and my sisters Mrs Barratt was at least a hundred years old. I see her now, petite and tidy with fading blue eyes matching her wrap-around pinafore. Her hair, 'as white as the driven snow', was neatly plaited and pinned around her small dainty head. Mum said Mrs B was 'a bit on the bewildered side' and I suppose these days she'd have Senile Dementia. To us though, she was just a whispered, 'Barmy Barratt from Next Door'.

I like to think she rather enjoyed having our noisy family close by. Our predecessor, Mrs Fudge had 'kept herself to herself', and after many short shrifts and rude rebuffs, even the bewildered Mrs B knew when to stop tap, tap, tapping on the window.

Anyway, Mrs Fudge died, and as our name was next on the Council Transfer List, we moved over to the posh side of the street - from 122 to 151. Our new home was a huge improvement - only one flight of stairs, a front room, living room, and, luxury of luxuries, an inside toilet!

For a while Mrs Barratt seemed unaware of Mrs Fudge's demise and our presence. She never looked our way when she was pegging out her smalls. I think it was April, the Easter holidays, when she spoke to us for the first time, "What time do you think the egg man will come? I just fancy a soft boiled egg for my tea."

We kids hadn't a clue what she was on about, but then Mum came out. "Oh hello. Mrs Barratt isn't it? Today's Friday dear, the Egg Man comes on Tuesdays. Fred the Fishman comes on Fridays and he'll certainly be here today as it's Good Friday. Everyone has fish on Good Friday don't they?"

Mrs B looked as bemused as we were about Fishy Fridays and Eggy Tuesdays, but she recognised a kindly voice. That was the start of the tap, tap, tapping.

These cries for help ranged from, "Is it going to rain today Mrs Brown?" to "There's a funny smell in my kitchen, what should I do?" The latter usually meant she'd turned on a gas ring and forgotten to light it. We were always happy to help.

Every Wednesday without fail she had a visitor - Doris. While Mrs Barratt was a bit doolally tap, Doris was as sharp as a tack. She had an ugly gait due to a 'tubercular hip' in childhood, but that didn't stop her limping the four miles to Mrs Barratt's each week to save on bus fares.

She always stayed three hours precisely, enough time to give the house a thorough fettling and stock up the larder. Then they'd sit down with a cup of tea, to reminisce about their time, 'in service'.

It wasn't long before Mum was invited in for a cuppa. There she discovered that Mrs Barratt had been housekeeper to a posh family in London, when Doris was a lowly housemaid. This hierarchy was still apparent, Mrs B was very bossy to Doris, who just accepted, and expected it.

Mrs Barratt had a skinny tortoiseshell cat called Henry. We girls loved Henry, but it soon became clear it was either feast or famine for Henry chez Barratt. Mrs B either fed him continuously or not at all. On the 'not at all' days he would cry piteously at our back door, so we persuaded Mum to add 2 tins of Co-op Cat meat to our Friday shopping list. That solved the problem; he became accustomed to getting his grub at our house on starvation days and it was gratifying to see him becoming nicely plump.

But back to the tap, tap, tapping on that hot August Sunday. It was Dad's turn for Mrs Barratt duties.

"Hello Mrs B. Everything alright?"

"Oh yes Mr Brown - it's just so exciting though. It's my cat, Henry, I do believe he's having kittens! I wonder if the girls would like to come and see?"

We arrived in Mrs Barratt's larder just in time for the birth of Henry's third slimy, skinny kitten. Our eyes were like saucers, and poor Judith our younger sister who was always squeamish - nearly fainted and fled back to 151.

After the shock wore off though, we were delighted with this neighbouring feline family. Like most little girls we loved all animals, and quickly became more and more entranced by their development and Henry's maternal skills. Then one of us, probably me, said, "I thought it was only mums who fed babies with them nipply things, not dads."

Mum and Dad looked at each other, eyebrows raised then Dad said. "Girls, I reckon you need to think of another name for Henry. He's not a boy, she's a girl. How about Henrietta?"

So Mother Henrietta she became, and I was delighted to follow the scrawny little scraps' progress. Every day after school I visited the new family. My favourite was kitten number three, and I spent hours pleading with Mum and Dad to let me keep it when the time to leave Henrietta. The pleas were all in vain because of Rex, our Alsatian cross. He was legendary in the neighbourhood for his hatred of all things feline. I'd never pretended to liked Rex much, but now I positively hated him.

They'd be about ten days old when Wednesday

arrived, and I went to school happily, secure in the knowledge that Henrietta would be fed after Doris's foray to the co-op. I got home around 4, and as usual for a Wednesday, there was a note leaning against the biscuit tin: "I'm next door with Mrs B and Doris, get yourself a ginger nut and a drink of milk. Come round if you want duck." Mum always said that, but I usually avoided these little gatherings like the plague.

I had no interest in the boring reminiscences about their time in service in the posh house. Mum however, being a huge Catherine Cookson fan, hung on to their every word. This particular Wednesday was different though and I was round there in a heart-beat. I'd grown so attached to the kittens and never missed an opportunity to see them.

To my delight their eyes were open and I swear Kitty 3 stared straight at me. I was so tempted to pick her up for a cuddle. Then I noticed Henrietta's warning glare, and realised it would be a very bad idea, so I settled for just watching them.

Although I knew that the vile, cat-hating Rex meant I couldn't have a kitten, it didn't stop me daydreaming about it. I decided my 'Kitty 3' couldn't be a boy, she was far too pretty - I even deliberated over what I'd call her - would she be Tabitha or Catherine? I thought a name associated with cats was a very clever, original idea. I was certain that Tabitha/Catherine and I would be the very best of friends, just like Suzie Smith in my Bunty comic. Her devoted cat Katy, shared all Suzies worries and never left her side. They were the best of friends.

Suddenly I jolted from this idyllic reverie by an imperious."Oh by the way, Doris, before you go, get that Dolly tub out. It's time to get rid of those kittens again, and while you're there shove Henry in as well this time.

I'm tired of all this messy drowning business every few months. Do be sure to give them all a good ponching, there's a dear."

And then, "Mrs Brown, I wonder if your girls would like to come and watch? I do believe they've always had a soft spot for Henry..."

My sisters and I were mortified and chose not to accept this invitation. We never spoke to Mrs Barrett. ever again - she didn't seem to notice though.

I cried and cried for a week.

The Earth Moved

Jennifer was loved up. She knew from the moment he hopped towards her that Jake Blackbird was THE ONE. Drop dead gorgeous or what? That bright orange beak, sleek glossy feathers and a tail to die for. Ooh and those eyes, a bird could drown in them.

They were great together, although Jake's reputation flew before him. Rumour had it he'd even done some bird. He certainly thought he was cock of the walk, but Jenny could handle that, and soon pecked him into shape if he ever hopped over the mark.

Before long Jenny felt broody.

'But duck,' said Jake, 'that's all well and good, but we've nowhere to live.'

'Well, find somewhere then, what are you a man or a mouse?' she trilled, hormonally irrational, 'and incidentally, I'm not a duck I'm a blackbird, in case you hadn't noticed.'

'Okay, okay, don't get your feathers in a flurry; I'll sort it, right? And for the record I'm a blackbird too, not a man or a flippin' mouse!'

The two black lovebirds planned their dream nest. They searched everywhere for a suitable garden and eventually plumped for one where they'd enjoyed many a full English over the winter. Jake's beak watered at the memory of the bacon rind and fat balls – '*mmmm scrumptious.*' Truth be told, it was this thought that tipped the scales for him.

They did an aerial 'recce' for suitable plots, and decided on a particularly lush conifer. It was conveniently close to the feeding table and they'd only spotted a couple of 'nose-in-the-air' moggies passing through. There was an old gardener who trudged by to his vegetable patch, but as they'd noticed him supplying the bacon rind and fat balls, they knew he meant them no harm. Sometimes there was a yappy little dog with him, and Jenny groused about this. Jake though, (thinking of the bacon rind and fat balls) said,

'You are a silly goose, all dogs are birdbrains and this one is especially dumb and useless. It's all bark and no bite.'

So they set to work. Jenny scavenged furiously, maternally eager to make the perfect home for the babies she so longed for. Jake half-heartedly helped with this sourcing of materials, but some of the rubbish he brought back, caused Jenny much exasperation.

'You silly old coot, what use are nub ends and ring pulls?' she admonished gently.

'Soz,' Jake said, and then, 'You're like a magpie at finding the right stuff Jen, but I know all about nest building so I'll be Project Manager, I'm much more useful in a, ahem, supervisory capacity.'

Jenny agreed to this lofty title a little doubtfully, and managed to peck her tongue when the avian 'Project Manager', perched on a high branch, crowed about his nest building prowess. Her beak twitched with amusement.

'I know it's taking a long while Jen,' he said, when she moaned about her tiredness and tatty talons, 'but you know, my little chickadee, if a job's worth doing, it's worth doing well. This is called teamwork; don't you think I'm knackered too duck? But we're nearly there.'

Eventually their home was complete and Jenny enjoyed flapping around putting the finishing touches to the nursery. She whistled contentedly, oblivious to Jake's absence, so she was surprised and touched when he later appeared with a beak full of fluffy brown fur.

'Nothing but the best for my little cocks,' he said, puffing out his chest proudly.

'Or hens,' tweeted Jenny blushing. 'Where did you get it from Jake?'

'Oh, you know me Jen,' Jake said, tapping his beak and winking, 'always on the look out for the main chance. Nothing but the best for my bird. I spotted the old gardener brushing the yappy dumb dog and noticed tufts of fur clinging to the grass, and I thought to myself, *'Perfick, my Jen'll love this for our nippers' nursery.'*

Jenny gulped back the lump in her throat and blinked away happy tears.

I'm so lucky, he's going to be a wonderful dad. First he finds the ideal plot for our new-build, then puts his Project Manager expertise into action, and now he's taking care of our brood before they even arrive. They broke the shell with my Jake.' She pecked him lovingly, while Jake preened with pride.

They moved in that evening and, so weary they fell asleep immediately. The dawn chorus woke them and with gritty, sluggish eyes they joined the throng... 500 ish.

It was the usual bun fight. Each morning was the same, everyone vying to make the most noise, tugs of war over the squelchiest worms, and tittle-tattle from busybody hens.

As Jenny foraged for food and nattered to her neighbours, she thought, *My beak overfloweth,* and glanced lovingly to Jake who was twittering to the dozen with his best pal Bernie.

'I reckon all my birthdays have come at once Bern,'

Jake chirruped excitedly, 'I've pulled the coolest chick around, my Jen's a right goer, let me tell you, but she's a grafter too. She got a bit carried away on the nest building front, but once I'd put her straight on the finer technicalities – well you've seen our new place, need I say more? Anyway for a young bird she's not half bad; and we've got all this lovely nosh; grubs, berries; and have you tasted those worms, cock? Talk about la crème de la crème. You'll have to come over in winter too, the old gardener serves a mean bacon and fat ball full English!'

Having eaten their fill and exchanged all the gossip the birds flew their separate ways. Jenny and Jake were still tired and, as Jake kept reminding her, they had some unfinished business at home. Later, nestling together, Jenny was appalled to see Jake scoffing bacon rind.

'Jake Blackbird, how romantic is this? We fly home to christen our new nest and all you can do is eat.'

'Come on Jen Hen, I need to keep my pecker up now don't I? said Jake through his greasy beak, 'come here and let's make beautiful baby blackbirds.'

Suddenly the earth moved, but not in the way Jennifer had romantically anticipated. There was a terrific noise below; the branches trembled with deafening rumbles. Jenny squawked and buried her head under Jake's wing.

'What is it, what is it Jake, is it an earthquake? Oh my God we'll be shaken out of the nest in a minute.'

'I'll have look, chicken,' replied Jake sounding much braver than he felt.

Under the tree he could see the old gardener was responsible for the horrendous noise. He was pushing a dirty smelly machine around and grass flew everywhere.

Jake went back to the nest and tried to reassure Jenny, although he could barely make himself heard. Jenny however was beyond hysterical.

'I can't stay here, Jake, I just can't, I'll die of fright, and what a place to rear our little chicks. It's no good we'll have to up twigs and find somewhere safer. If you don't come I'll go it alone.'

Jake didn't need any persuading, he was freaked out of his feathers anyway. They waited until dark, then did a moonlight flit, Jake with his face full of fat ball and bacon rind and Jenny with a beak full of fur from the dumb yappy dog.

She was sentimental like that.

The Initiation – An Apprentice's tale

They called it work experience, but it was more than that.
The gangly youth was nervous as he donned his safety
hat.
John's first day on the building site; and he was just a
scholar,
New overalls that chafed his thighs, he missed his tie and
collar.

His mummy made his pack-up, mmm corned beef on
white sliced bread,
A flask of tea, some Parkin, and a kiss upon his head.
The site was full of brawny men, unshaven with tattoos,
Poor Johnny still had bum fluff, and his mum still chose
his shoes.

The roguish navvies recognised this nervous sitting duck
He looked around with heavy heart, *Oh crikey, just my
luck!*
The first trick was an old one; a well-used builder's
wheeze,
They sent him off to B & Q, to get some elbow grease.

He came back empty handed, embarrassed at this gaffe,
Expected trouble from the blokes but all they did was
laugh.
The day became a nightmare with their jokes and 'funny'
tricks
And then disaster struck as John was lugging round some
bricks.

"Oh damn and blast!" he yelled in pain, "can someone lend a hand?
I've gone and done my back in now and I can't hardly stand."
They carefully pulled him erect; he winced and whispered, "Thanks.
I'm sorry but I have to rest, I can't lift up those planks."

His new "mates" held a quick pow-wow, knew someone with the knack,
Who'd help him chill, relax him and forget his poor sore back.
She owned a massage parlour and her name was Big Eileen,
With innocence John said, "Yes please," Poor lad was oh so green.

He lay prostrate on shabby couch, soft towel hiding his bits
Oh wow, he thought with saucer eyes, she's got ginormous tits
She did a bit of pummelling but specialised in stroking
Excitement was too much for him; he thought he'd die from choking

She told him of her special deal and then John understood
She winked as she removed the towel revealing young manhood.
John's agony diminished, as he pulled Big Eileen down
And as her breasts enveloped him he thought he'd surely drown.

Emerging some time later, John blinked and shook his
head,
Big Eileen simply smiled at him as she lay there on the
bed
The lads at work all cheered him as he strode into the
yard
Erect he stood with shoulders back, feeling proper hard!

"Now then lad" his mother said, "tell me as best you may,
how was it down the builder's yard on this your first full
day?
John blushed as red as beetroot, and told as best you can,
How, leaving out Big Eileen, a boy becomes a man!

Dawn Raffle

I enjoyed working within and for the community for
many years as a Scheme Manager in Sheltered Housing,
until my retirement. I have always loved reading and now
I have found the time to write stories for others to enjoy.

The Gift

The shadows deepen and I fear the night,
Oh pity me, won't someone bring a light?
Memories crowd, unbidden, cruel and stark,
My cries unheeded, left here in the dark,
The air grows chill, my lonely heart takes fright.

He comes in silence, eyes so bleak and cold,
No signs of passion; love I'd hoped to hold.
I'd walked in glory, thought him to be true,
Then saw his other, fair with eyes bright blue.
The truth so clear - he loved only my gold.

So, crushed, I stole away, my heart in two,
My anger told me what I'd have to do.
His birthday party came - I planned with care,
Surprise, surprise, when just we two were there!
"My gift, my love, I picked these out for you."

He gasped - two blue eyes looking up at him,
As pretty as the box I'd placed them in.
Shocked, he stumbled back in grief and horror
Weeping tears of pain and utmost sorrow.
My hurt avenged, I wore a mirthless grin.

And now I'm locked away alone, insane,
He comes and goes whilst here I must remain.
I see his eyes each night, so stern and fell,
Unblinking as I cringe in my dark cell,
How can he be so cruel yet again?

Chris Rawlins

I'm a retired publisher from the academic world on both sides of the Atlantic, with a second home in Florida. I enjoy writing while not travelling or busy with other activities such as volunteer work, gardening at an allotment, watching sports events or doing grand-parenting duties.

Treasured Island

Much of the British Isles was in a mess in 1946. World War 2 had ended the previous year with monumental damage everywhere. While England and southern Scotland had suffered the most from Nazi bombings, the Scottish highlands and islands were crippled in a variety of other ways.

Communities in such villages as Kyleakin, the gateway to the Isle of Skye from the mainland, had lost many of their men who had served in the armed forces. Others had been forced to operate in other parts of their country, or even England, and were reluctant to return. There were much greater opportunities elsewhere offering faster growth.

One exception was Ian McCullough, a farmer's son. He had served at a naval base on the south coast of England. Ian's parents still lived in Kyleakin and he was thrilled at the prospect of returning home.

When he arrived back in 1946, he was saddened by what he saw. Most of the houses were standing, but where were the villagers? Many of Ian's younger friends had been killed in action. What remained was a much older village population, with several homes left empty and in need of repair.

Ian soon decided to make Kyleakin a tourist attraction for all of Skye and to improve the local economy. His father, Bruce, was so supportive of Ian's ideas that they agreed to establish a business partnership to help Skye's tourism. They realised that the history, scenery and mountains of Skye could attract people but it needed many more visitors. Kyleakin is the starting point for most tourists because of its close proximity to the mainland, and its regular ferry service. Once there, they would need feeding and somewhere to stay.

Bruce knew a young couple, Douglas and Morag

Ferguson, living outside Skye's largest town, Portree. He persuaded them to buy an old house in Kyleakin, which they converted into a four-bedroom guesthouse with a dining room. Others in the village also began to provide bed-and-breakfast accommodation under Ian and Bruce's direction, and some went even further by re-establishing a couple of village shops. The owner of the village pub was inspired to modernize and introduce an eating area, and by the summer of 1948 visitors to Skye had somewhere to sleep, eat, drink, and shop.

However, those tourists without a car were often disappointed. Public transport was scarce and there was relatively little to do, except walking and climbing. Bruce and Ian had separate ideas as to how they might enhance holiday plans for tourists.

Bruce's plan was entirely accidental. He heard that a local bus company on the mainland in Mallaig was investing in a fleet of about ten new vehicles. Seizing the opportunity, he persuaded the manager to sell him one of their old buses for a very reasonable price. Bruce drove it triumphantly back to Kyleakin via the Armadale ferry.

He found a young villager to drive it all over Skye, and they were in business! This allowed tourists without cars to explore Portree, Broadford, Staffin, and Dunvegan Castle. Some even went out climbing in the Cuillin Hills or just walking to admire the beautiful coastal scenery.

The service became very popular after it was advertised in the local tourist guides and by the Scottish Tourist Board, and Skye tourism began to grow steadily, helping both the local economy and the McCullough business.

Ian had another idea. Fishing had always been one of his many interests, so he planned to develop fishing trips for visitors. This would enable them to take part in something more active than being driven around in a bus; and they might even return with some fish.

He managed to repair an old boat which could hold up to six anglers. Some of his early trips included a number of tourists who complained that they had paid good money for a trip but had caught nothing. Since these fishing trips had all been north of Kyleakin, Ian decided to try in the southern part of the island.

On one of his first trips, Ian's boat was just north of Armadale when one tourist caught a canvas bag with only a drink carton inside it. Whereupon Ian gave him and the other clients a tutorial on how to catch fish such as pollack, wrasse, mackerel, or even tope, using lures. He then gave them a demonstration – and to their amusement brought to the surface another canvas bag!

Unlike the first, though, this one was quite heavy. Intrigued, Ian delved inside. He was astonished to find several leather pouches and boxes in surprisingly good condition. Quickly he opened them, only to discover they were full of jewellery; a hoard of diamonds, rings, necklaces, bracelets, bangles and much more. Ian couldn't believe his luck.

Ever the opportunist, Ian took the treasure to a jeweller in Edinburgh, an old Army chum, who bought the lot for £25,000, no questions asked. Ian was suddenly wealthy, and this windfall enabled the McCullough family to develop a visitor centre, and to secure the future of Skye as a world-renowned tourist destination.

The McCullough Centre, just outside Kyleakin on a height overlooking the sea, became a landmark and a reminder that Skye is indeed a 'Treasured Island'.

Cindy Rossiter

A successful Hucknall business woman for the last two decades running my own image consultancy, my feet are firmly planted in reality and my head in the stars. Lover of life, I enjoy people, poetry and prose, yoga, travel and interior design.

Count Your Blessings

Cats dead
Wife's upset
House remortgaged
To pay the vet

Children moaning
Inheritance spent
Bank foreclosing
We'll have to rent

In a shoebox
It's not so bad
Reminds me of
When I was a lad

Pig's trotter
Ox's tail
Scrag end of beef
And Adam's ale

Landlord livid
We've paid him nowt
Bruise now vivid
Where he gave me a clout

Wife ran off
Back home to mum
Couldn't face another day
In this slum

Been evicted
On the streets
Pavement pounding
Is killing my feet

Hostels are great
Soup and bread
A safe haven
To rest my head

No room at the inn
So a night with the stars
Breathing fresh air
And looking for Mars

My luck has changed
I've found a stray
She doesn't mind
Where we stay

She curls in my arms
Warming my chest
No thermals needed
I'm truly blessed!

From Here to Infirmity

The writing's on the wall, I'd say
it's all downhill from here.
I don't need to count my birthdays,
the signs are crystal clear.

The sagging chin, the drooping breasts,
a thickening at my waist,
the need to apply more make-up,
I can no longer go bare-faced.

Where are my specs? What's that you say?
What's happened to my hair?
It seems to have migrated,
and now it's everywhere.

Gum disease, incontinence
and the trouble with my hip,
my knees, my joints, my arthritis,
I may have to use a stick.

It appears that I have bunions
growing bigger day by day,
and fluctuating hormones;
night sweats seem here to stay.

I know what day of the week it is,
as well as the month and year,
but quizzes are a nightmare,
instant recall's gone I fear.

There's one thing keeps me going,
it's a matter of degree.
My best friend's five years older,
and she's much worse than me.

Snake in the Grass

Snakily he slithers his lean length
around the lonely ladies,
long-term lover forgotten.
Despite his pole position,
delightful den,
creature comforts,
off he slides
recoiling from suburbia.
Relentless -
he fixes on his prey.

Alone,
a good catch, lovely lair.
Weaving his way around her heart,
he quickly penetrates her defences,
it doesn't take him long
to scale the stairs.
There's stolen hours in his den,
early morning trysts in the park
lying in the long grass -
with the sun warming his back.

His pleasure intensifies
as the risks mount.
So simple to deceive his mate
when gliding through the days
unchecked.
Alibis?
Lies come easily to those of forked tongue
Comes the moment,
his deviousness is discovered and
white-lipped he finds himself
No match for his wife's venom.

Fierce-fanged she bites back.
The wound is deep – all is lost
Perhaps his lover will have him?
Alas!
His hypnotic hold is broken
and she slips silently away.
Spitting, he slithers on.
'Cold blooded' he hisses
'like my wife.
Both reptiles!'

The Shoes

Silvery, glittery, diamante on black.
High, high heels and so much style.
No wonder she put them on the table
Amidst the place settings, the balloons, the flowers.
They stood proud.

The guests were noisy.
I'd asked for quiet, and all she was doing
was trying to get it for me.
At the time I thought, "You can't use your shoes as a gavel!
They could break! They could be ruined!
And it won't work anyway."

It didn't -
 an insignificant tap against the din,
 but she'd shown everyone
 how beautiful they were.

"I fell off my shoe dancing"
she wailed later that night,
displaying her injured ankle for me to inspect
and clutching her shoe.
And yet still I didn't rise to it.

And then, on the phone the next day
"I fell off my shoe – did you see?"
 "I did see" I said
"and by the way, I saw your shoes.
They're beautiful, I absolutely love them!"
"Yes…Prada" she sighed.

Unfurled

A moveable feast
A fleeting thing
What is happiness?
A bird on the wing

A transitory moment
A sense of peace
Soft intake of breath
A sighing release

Ability to balance
On uneven ground
To perceive beauty
All around

Emotions touched
Brain well fed
Love of learning
A steady head

Flying high
Towards the light
Self fulfilment
Swooping flight

Blissful night
Living Long
Dawn chorus
Uplifting song

A sense of being
At one with the world
In life's sunshine
Wings unfurled

Sam Taylor

Yorkshire born, pierced and tattooed freak who likes art, history and the great outdoors, and who's lived in Bagthorpe for 20 years.

Gone With the Tsar

To whom these woods belong, I used to know
On whose head jewels and gold once sat, now;
He will never know I trespassed here
To watch white-dusted trees bowed down with snow.

Horse tussles, jingles, skittish with our fear
Of such unlawful loitering so near;
The Royal house who'd quickly have our head
On a spike in darkest winter forest drear.

My head held high, for all I did the deed,
I laid my victims in such silent woods,
Mother and children, corseted with jewels
Sacrificed for the cause, the greater good.

Guns rattle not, breath billows in the cold,
Hangs like ghostly shadows round my head,
The only other sound's the baying wolves
For the blood of a heartless killer not quite dead.

The wood's so lovely, silent, deep and old;
Their blood's on my hands as they lie cold
Will you remember me, when this tale's told?
Will you remember me, when this tale's told?

I Shall Walk Alone

To the valley of death I walk alone,
A life unlived my careless day has been,
Aboard the ferry while other voices drone.

From this olive-groved countryside I'd grown,
I went to war as a boy barely sixteen,
Leaving my love and family, to walk alone.

I died in the field loving you my sweet, sweet Joan,
Mustard gas blinded us to enemies – unseen
Among the trees, guns spoke with deadly tone.

Our souls wait by the river Styx for Charon,
The ferry man, gold on our eyes in lien.
I leave this world as I was born, alone.

My life like a candle in the wind was blown
Out as it poor played its little scene;
I listen to the whispers as other souls drone.

Now at rest I lay my youthful bones,
Small remnants of the headstrong boy I'd been,
And to the valley of death I walk alone,
Aboard the ferry while other voices drone.

Mike Wareham

I was an English teacher in East Midlands comprehensive schools for 33 years. Then I saw the light and started writing stories and poems instead, completing a degree in Creative writing at Nottingham University, which I found much more fun than marking! I still teach – film, creative writing and literature – but only to people who've left school. I love playing the guitar and singing Country and Blues.

Circling Melangell

The circle of hills, grail,
bowls low to the circle of yews.
In the church the shrine of St. Melangell.

In this round churchyard,
Monacella, Virgin Moon,
did you lift up your skirts

to let the Great Hare in?
Did you feel God's heart
beating there?

Our Lady of the wood-cat,
is this 'thin place',
where the yews are older than Christ,

the threshold to heaven?

Beware, says the white pheasant in the wood.
Beware, beware, says the loping dew-flirt hare.

The moors gyre, spill
 in a white linn over the waterfall lip
and the pool brims.

I circle it.
I brim with it.
I feel its thinness,

the world beyond this world
time present and time past
stretching before and after.

Beware, says the white pheasant in the wood.
Beware, beware says the loping dew-flirt hare.

In the early 7th century, Melangell, the daughter of an Irish king, fled to a remote spot at the head of the Tanat Valley in the Berwyn Mountains in North Wales. Here she lived a solitary life until the Prince of Powys went there hunting and a frightened hare took refuge in her dress. The Prince's dogs were subdued, and, deeply impressed, he gave her the valley to create a sanctuary. Ever since Pennant Mellangell has been a place of pilgrimage and Melangell remains the patron saint of hares.

Dog-Retch Billy

They call me Dog-Retch Billy, kids on our estate. I
hate them. They call me Scab Billy too. That's because I
were only one on estate as kept working during '84 strike.
They still all hate me for that round here.

Reason they called me Dog-Retch Billy were
because I used to have one but they took it off me. Great
big pit-bull mastiff he were. No-one gave me no shit
when I had him with me. I used to take him down Ponds
for a walk. There's these ponds – well lakes really – near
where I live, and fields where you can go. The ponds are
where drift mine used to be, where they've all filled up
with water and there's a sort of country park. I used to
take him down there, like I say, for a walk. I like to go
bird-watching there, too, take my binoculars.

I let him off lead once because all these Canada
Geese were out on grass, feeding. I hate Canada Geese,
there's too many of them, they shouldn't be in this
country, they keep all proper British geese away and eat
all grass and shit everywhere so grass gets all slimy and
you fall over in it. So I thought maybe my dog could
catch one and kill it and I could have had it for dinner.

But as soon as I let him off leash all geese just took
off and dog were running all over shop and when I called
him he wouldn't come back. That's when these two kids
– well teenagers, a girl and a boy – come round the corner
and they've got this little mongrelly terrier thing that is
off lead and it's right snappy and my dog goes up to it.
Well my dog wants to play but this terrier, it's that
snappy my dog gets a right radge on, like, and picks it up

in her teeth and starts shaking it.

Of course these two kids were going ape-shit at me, saying Get it off! Get it off! and I tried but I couldn't as dog were too strong for me , and then when boy tried to pull it off he got bit really bad. Pit-bull mastiff jaws are mega strong so terrier weren't a pretty sight when my dog had finished with it; it were all mangled and bloody and that were it for him. Them kids got me reported, so I lost dog and it got put down and now I can't have dog at all. But they shouldn't have had their dog off lead anyroad up. It being that snappy, they should have known. They're like all kids nowadays – pig-ignorant, don't care.

There's a lot of kids come down Ponds. They go fishing and that, for gudgeon and roach in river that joins the ponds, even though it's private, trespassing. It's the other kids that get me worse, though, older ones. Bunch of chavs. They're always coming down Ponds with cans of extra strong lager and alcopops and bottles of white cider and that, and they sit on benches and make a fucking noise, laughing and shouting and snogging and other disgusting stuff. They always shout at me and call me names like I said 'cos their dads were all NUM and I were UDM. Like them two with the dog, the terrier. His dad, little ginger haired shit he is, were shop steward of pit when they came out on strike. He's one of worst for calling me. 'Ey up Scabbie Billy,' he'll shout at me, all sarky like. He comes down with his girl and get up to all sorts. He puts his tongue down her throat and his hand up her skirt. Fucking slag, she is. Mind you, it's funny, she's not from round here originally. She lives on the estate they've built on old pit top – all double garages and posh gardens with conservatories and that. Her dad drives a Lexus and her mum works in town in an office I reckon. I see her mum with her executive case going to catch

Robin Hood line into Nottingham. Girl goes with her in a green blazer with red edges, from that posh girls' school in Nottingham, Hollygirt. I've seen ads on the back of buses.

After I lost dog I still carried on going down Ponds just to see what were going off. Anyway, this girl's family had just moved into village, and they used to bring their golden labrador in the back of their Lexus and walk it there. They had this long plastic thing with a cup on one end and they used to put a ball in it and then they'd throw ball with this thing and it would go fucking miles. I were really impressed. So I went to pet shop in Kirkby, Perfect Pets, and I bought one, A Dog Ball Launcher it were called. Black plastic. I took it to Ponds and I could sling big pebbles a hundred yards, at least. I were that chuffed with it that I changed its name and called it The Sling and made it a leather case. I were always going down there, or on waste ground by the old mineral railway, practising. I'd set up bottles for targets and then walk away a hundred yards and try to hit them. After a while I got really good. I used to fill them with red-coloured water. It were great when they exploded, all red, like blood.

It were then that I thought, Why not try and kill one of them Canada Geese? So one day, real early in morning, I went down to Ponds before anyone were there. There were all geese, feeding on grass, and it were all dewy and misty and quiet. I got The Sling out of its case, put big heavy round pebble into it, aimed, and then, whoosh! Pebble went straight into geese and thwack, right into side of one I were aiming for. All geese then went honking into sky like klaxons and flew over my head really near, so I could hear wings beating, quite scary. I went over to goose I'd hit and it were all bloody where stone had gone in. But it were still flapping around a bit as it weren't quite dead. I got it and tried to wring its neck like I saw on film once, but it didn't work. So then I stood on its neck with one foot and stamped on its head with other. Brains all come out then and it died. I took it home and gutted it and plucked it and put it in freezer. I'll have it for Christmas dinner.

It were about that time when kids on estate started calling me Dog-Fetch Billy, or sometimes just Dog-Fetch. It's 'cause they'd seen me with The Sling, practising and that. And they all knew about my mastiff that were took away. Where's yer dog, Scab Billy? And then Where's yer dog, Dog-Fetch? And then they started to change it. Where's yer dog, Dog-Retch? Where's yer dog, Dog-Retch? Yeah, they called me that all time after a bit. I didn't like that.

That's about when I found this old bird hide on one of Ponds, hidden in woods. To get to it you have to go over marsh on wooden walkway, but walkway's rotten and dangerous, so they've fenced it off. They padlocked hide as well. I knew a way round fence and through marsh and I cut their lock off and put on my own. I started going there a lot, got a proper scope – started bird-watching proper, got to know all birds. It's surprising how many different birds there are just on this one lake. Coots, moorhens, mallards, grebes, pochard, the lot. I used to love going down that old hide – could spend all day there – even took a Camping Gaz stove to make tea. Sometimes I'd take a magazine with me as well, Just 18 or Naughty Neighbours ,'cos I like pictures.

One day I were watching lake through binoculars, enjoying peace and quiet. Suddenly, on other side of the lake, I could see something, two people, moving through undergrowth. This were well weird as nobody ever came there usually, it being hard to get to and dead overgrown. As they came nearer they pushed their way onto a little tongue of land that jutted out into lake. At the end of this tongue of land were a little grassy bank with an old stone bench that been there forever, by looks of it, and that's where they sat down. They were completely hidden from view, except from me, and they couldn't see me, of course, as I was in the hide. I were gobsmacked -- it were that little red haired shit and the posh girl – the ones as had terrier, the ones that got my dog put down. When these two turned up I felt really weird.

They were only about fifty yards away and I could see them really well through scope, like they were right in front of me. The girl had curly blond hair and a flowery dress on so you could see her legs. They sat there for a while, snogging and that and then he started to put his hands under her dress and she had her arms round his neck, pulling him to her, like. Things went from bad to worse then, as then she got on top of him, sat astride, like, and he pulled her dress down and he were kissing her tits, and she were kissing his face and like I say, it were like watching it on T.V. with the scope, even though there were no sound. Well, then he squirmed from underneath her and took his jeans off and then pretty soon he were on top of her and I could see his bum going up and down and her legs were round him and he were on top of her, kissing her and kissing her and his bum were going at her, going at her, so as pretty soon I couldn't take it no more. I had to stop them. So I thought, I know, I'll give them a scare, little shits, and I got The Sling out of its case and a huge great pebble and I went out on bank next to hide and I aimed and I slung pebble and it went whoosh right across lake and it hit little red-haired fucker right in the head. That's stopped him, I thought, as now his bum had stopped going at her and he were lying on top of her. I

188

went back to the hide then and looked at them through scope and I could see it all in close-up. His head were all bloody and the blood had gone all over lass's chest. She were lying there underneath him and he were dead still, but I thought I could hear her screaming as her mouth were moving. After a bit she pushed him off and stood looking at him, shaking and screaming. I didn't really know what to do -- it were a bit of a shock, all this, now. Eventually, I couldn't stand it and decided to leave them to it. I packed scope up, I locked door and I went home. Serves them right, though, the little shits.

Exile

My Nainie took me gathering wool today.
We pulled it from the gorse, the brambles, hawthorn,
barbed wire where the sheep had rubbed.

She showed me the dykes
that divided the fields in the old days –
you can see their ghosted outlines
from across the valley.
She said the old people grew
oats and barley up here
when it was sunny and warm
in the old days
before the cold times came
before they left the land.

She showed me the *caer* on the mynedd
the hill fort marked Roman Fort on the map.
But my Nainie says the old people built it,
long before the Romans came.
Or the English.
Before they left the land.

We took the wool in carrier bags
back to the old farmhouse.
We carded it into fine cirrus clouds
made rolags of stormy cumulus,
drew the thread out like a miracle
span it and rolled it into soft firm balls.

They lay like eggs in her willow basket –
drumlins.

She told of the winter of '47
when she and Taid were stranded here for weeks
like sheep in a snow drift.
How he started on her, isn't it?
But then he started on my mum
and she couldn't put up with that.

One day, after the thaw,
he was drunk with whisky.
She took my mum and escaped.
They never went back to the land.

And now, we sit here spinning,
Wool-gathering in the long evenings.
I've come back to the land.

Girl in Snow

She gave it me the morning they sent her away –
a little girl in a snowstorm ball, it was.
Each day I shake it and she's lost again.

I didn't go to see her off –
hid in the barn, ashamed I was
for what we'd done.

I saw her through the window, though,
head held high, looking round, proud,
as she got in the car with the snow coming down.

We'd had it since we were little,
a gift from an uncle but it was always hers,
the black-haired girl in the snow.

Sometimes, when the frost curdled on our window
we'd sleep together
like two lambs in a snow drift.

Now, when it snows, I always see her,
getting into the car
and I shake the snow-storm ball

and she's lost again.

Rowan Berries

I stood in the parlour window gazing
through the misty panes. Watching, I was,
for my uncle's black Morris Oxford, coming to pick me
up.
Taking me to a nice hostel, they said.

I remember my little suitcase;
my little wellies by the door, waiting;
my flowered frock –
slipping my hand under to feel my big tummy.

Da was up on the Mynydd, wouldn't come down.
Bryn was hiding in the barn.
Aunt Jane, thin lipped, was in the kitchen,
making a thermos and crab-paste sandwiches.

I didn't know whose it was. Was it Bryn's,
who used to take me to the sweet-scented
hayloft, after the milking was over?
A mortal sin, they said it was, with your brother.

Or was it red-haired Tecwyn, who took me to
the ferny pools beneath the waterfalls,
where we'd swim, white-limbed,
then lie beneath the bracken together?

At last the Morris splashed into the farmyard,
the dogs dancing round it, crazy.
I remember the smell of the
red leather seats as I got in.

I remember the red berries on the rowan trees
hanging over the track, at the last gate.
They are there now, as I open the gate again,
twenty years later, my son's hand in mine, red haired.

The Housemartins

The housemartins came here,
every year, each April.
Sleek black-blue and white, they swooped
to the stream that splashes through the sedge
for pecks of mud from the clayey banks;

slathered up the holes in last year's nests
that clustered in the eaves,
each one a perfect semi-sphere
moulded from stippled mud.

Weeks later five beaks gaped from every nest.
The parents careered the valley,
scooped flies in beakfuls for them.

We held out candles, after dark,
from bedroom windows
to where they nested in the eaves,
peered at them cheeping softly to each other in their nests.
All night we heard them as if in their dreams.

When midsummer broods all fledged
the air was hectic with commotions of martins;
darting in entwined flights
a twittering swarm
in our little valley.

Last year, they did not come –
blown off course by Saharan storms?
This year, again, they have not come:
the nests are washed away by winter rains.

I sit on the porch, summer silent now.
Only a willow warbler's song
trickles from the shivering aspen.